101 BEST
CARD GAMES
FOR CHILDREN

ALFRED SHEINWOLD

Illustrated by
DOUG ANDERSON

A Piccolo Book
Pan Books London and Sydney

Also available in this series

101 *Best Magic Tricks* Guy Frederick

First published in Great Britain 1958 by Nicholas Kaye Ltd
This edition published 1971 by
Pan Books Ltd, Cavaye Place, London SW10 9PG
ISBN 0 330 02796 4
8th printing 1975 (For Scholastic Publications Ltd.)
© Sterling Publishing Company Inc 1956

Printed in Great Britain by
Cox & Wyman Ltd, London, Reading and Fakenham

Contents

Contents

Introduction

My own experience makes me feel that *every* child will benefit from playing card games.

It is a healthy experience for a child to play with grown-ups as an equal; and to play with other children without noticing difference in age.

It is good for the child's character to get practice in losing without squawking and in winning without crowing. (Many adults could use some of this practice too!)

A young child can learn about numbers and easy arithmetic from a simple card game. A child of *any* age can exercise his brain by the logical thinking that is needed in the more advanced games.

Moreover, card games are *fun*. And this is the best of all reasons for teaching them to children.

My thanks are due to my old friend Geoffrey Mott-Smith, who worked with me on this book; and to his children for the many games we played together.

ALFRED SHEINWOLD

Publisher's Note

Throughout this book the author for preference uses the word 'deck' to the word 'pack' to describe a complete set of playing cards. Although now more commonly employed in the USA than in the United Kingdom, 'deck' has a long history of use for this purpose and was, indeed, at one period, more acceptable than 'pack' even in England.

Another two unusual words appearing frequently are 'meld' and 'ante'. The meaning of both will be clear from their context and a general explanation of 'meld' will be found in *Basic Rummy*.

1. For the Very Young . . .

These games are for children who are too young to think . . . and for grown-ups who would rather *not* think! Sometimes it's hard to tell whether the children or the grown-ups laugh harder!

PIG

This is a very hilarious game for children or for adults to play with children. Anybody can learn the game in two or three minutes, and one extra minute makes you an expert!

NUMBER OF PLAYERS: Three to thirteen. Five or six make the best game.

CARDS: Four of a kind for each player in the game. For example, five players would use twenty cards: four Aces, four Kings, four Queens, four Jacks, and four 10s. For six players you would add the four 9s.

THE DEAL: Any player shuffles and deals four cards to each player.

OBJECT: To get four of a kind in your own hand, or to be quick to notice it when somebody else gets four of a kind.

THE PLAY: Each player looks at his hand to see if he was dealt four of a kind. If nobody has four of a kind, each player puts some unwanted card face down on the table and passes it to the player at his left, receiving a card at the same time from the player at his right.

Each player looks at his hand as it appears with the newly-received card. If, still, nobody has four of a kind, each player once again passes a card to the left and gets a new card from the right.

The play is continued in this way until some player has four of a kind in his hand. That player stops passing or receiving cards since he is satisfied with his hand as it is. Instead of playing on, he puts his finger to his nose.

The other players must be quick to notice this, and each of them must stop passing in order to put a finger to his nose. The last player to put a finger to his nose is the *Pig*.

SKILFUL PLAY: In trying to put together four of a kind, you must usually start with a pair. For example, suppose you are dealt two Kings, one Queen, and one Ace. Keep the two Kings, and pass either the Queen or the Ace. As soon as you get another King, save all three of them, and pass your fourth card. Sooner or later your fourth King will come in.

Don't get so interested in looking for your own four of a kind that you are blind to what the other players are doing. Keep one eye on everybody else, particularly on those who look very eagerly at the cards they are receiving. The eager player probably has three of a kind and is just waiting for the fourth.

The best *Pig* player I know is a little girl who doesn't try very hard to make four of a kind. She always tries to look excited, and talks and squeals as she gets each card, just as though she had three of a kind. While doing all of this, she watches the other players to see which of them are interested in her and which are interested in their own hands.

She knows that the players who are interested in *her* have *bad* hands, but that those who are thinking about the *game* have *good* hands. So little Lisa knows which players to watch, and she is never caught!

DONKEY

This is the same game as *Pig*, except that when a player gets four of a kind he puts his hand face down on the table quietly instead of putting his finger to his nose. He still gets a card from his right and just passes that along to the left, leaving his four of a kind untouched on the table.

As each player sees what has happened, he likewise puts his hand down quietly. The idea is to keep up the passing and the conversation while some player plays on without realizing that the hand has really ended.

The last player to put his cards down loses the hand. This makes him a D. The next time he loses, he becomes a D-O. The third time, he becomes a D-O-N. This keeps on, until finally some player becomes a D-O-N-K-E-Y.

The D-O-N-K-E-Y loses the game, and the winner is the player who has the smallest number of letters.

DONKEY BUTTONS

This is the same game as Donkey, except that when a player gets four of a kind he shouts 'Donkey' and quickly grabs a button from the middle of the table. There is one button less than there are players, so the last player to grab doesn't get a button. He becomes a D, and the game continues in this way until somebody becomes a D-O-N-K-E-Y.

At the end of the game, the D-O-N-K-E-Y has to bray *'heehaw'* three times.

MY SHIP SAILS

NUMBER OF PLAYERS: Four to seven. Four or five players make the best game.

CARDS: Seven to each player, dealt one at a time in the usual way.

OBJECT: To get seven cards of the same suit.

THE PLAY: Each player looks at his hand and passes one card to the left, receiving at the same time one card from the right. The play goes on in the same way as in *Pig* or *Donkey*. The only difference is that you are trying to collect cards which all have the same suit instead of the same picture.

There are many different ways of ending a hand. When you get seven cards of the same suit, you may put your hand down immediately and sing out, 'My ship sails!' Another way is to say nothing but to put your finger to your nose as in *Pig*.

If it takes too long to finish a hand, try one of the shorter games – *My Bee Buzzes* or *My Star Twinkles*.

SKILFUL PLAY: Begin by trying to collect the suit that you have most of. For example, if you have four or five hearts, pass the other cards and try to collect more hearts.

The only time you have trouble is when some other player

tries to collect the same suit that you are collecting. To guard against this, try to collect a second suit if you don't have any luck with your first suit. If you can get three cards in a second suit, you can then start to pass the cards of your first suit and thus switch your plan.

For example, suppose you start with three hearts, two spades, one club, and one diamond. Keep passing the clubs and diamonds until you get another heart or another spade. If you get one more – or a third spade before any heart is passed to you, you should suspect that somebody else is saving the hearts. Your best bet is to break up your hearts and to try to get seven spades instead.

If you have four or more cards in the same suit, it doesn't pay to break. Sit tight and hope that one of the other players will break first and thus pass the cards that you need.

MY BEE BUZZES

This is the same as *My Ship Sails* except that you need only six cards of the same suit to end the hand. Each player gets seven cards, but needs only six cards in the same suit (and one odd card) to win the hand. It takes less time to finish a hand in this game than in *My Ship Sails*.

MY STAR TWINKLES

This is the same as *My Ship Sails* except that you need only five cards of the same suit (and two odd cards) to win a hand. In this game it takes only two or three minutes to play a hand.

THROUGH THE WINDOW

NUMBER OF PLAYERS: Three to thirteen – the more the merrier.

THE DEAL: Four cards to each player.

OBJECT: To win the most cards.

THE PLAY: The dealer begins by saying, 'I looked through the window, and saw—'. Just at this moment, and not before, he turns up one of his four cards so that all of the players can see it.

Each player (including the dealer) must try to say an animal or a thing beginning with the same letter of the alphabet as the card that has been turned up. For example, if the card is an Ace, you might call out, 'Ant', 'Alligator', or 'Ammunition', or anything else that begins with the letter A. If the card is a 9, you might call out, 'Newt', or 'Nut'.

The first player to call out a correct word takes the card and starts his pile of captured cards separate from the four cards that were dealt to him. Then the person at left of the dealer says, 'I looked through the window and saw—', turning up one of his cards. The game continues in the same way, in turn to the left, until all the cards originally dealt have been turned up and captured. Each person keeps his own pile of captured cards, and the one who captures the most wins the game. The captured cards have nothing to do with each player's original four cards, since each player had exactly four chances to turn up a card.

As soon as a word has been used to win a card, no player can use that same word again. For example, if you have used the word 'Stone' to capture a seven, neither you nor any other player can use the word 'Stone' to capture any other card beginning with an S.

THROUGH THE WIDE WINDOW

This is played exactly like *Through the Window*, except that when a card is turned, you must call out two words: an animal or an object, and a word describing that animal or object. For example, if a King is turned up, you might call out, 'Kind Kitten' or 'Kissable Kipper'. Any single word may be used more than once in the game However, no pair of words may be repeated. For example, if you call out 'Quivering Quail' on seeing a Queen, anybody may use the word 'Quivering' and anybody may use the word 'Quail' for another Queen, but nobody is allowed to use the two words together.

SKILFUL PLAY: A trick of playing this game successfully is to have a little stock of words that begin with the right letters. For example, you might be ready with the words Ant, Alligator, Anteater, Abacus, Apple, etc, when an Ace turns up. Similarly, you make a little list of words beginning with T for Two, Three, or Ten, and so on for the nine letters of the alphabet that begin the names of the playing cards. In the same way, you need a list of descriptive words, such as Active, Adult, Adorable, Affectionate, Agitated, etc, in the case of an Ace.

When grown-ups play with children, the best rule is to make the grown-ups use two words (a descriptive word as well as the object or animal), while the children need only one word.

CONCENTRATION

NUMBER OF PLAYERS: Any number at all – the more the merrier.

THE DEAL: Just spread the cards face down on a table. Don't bother to put them down neatly, but just jumble them up, making sure that no two cards overlap.

OBJECT: To capture pairs of cards. The player who captures the most pairs wins the game.

THE PLAY: Before play begins, each player should be told what his turn is. Thus each player knows whether he is first, second, third, etc.

The first player turns up any card and then turns up any other card. If the two cards match each other (for example, if they are two Aces, or two Kings, etc) the first player captures them as his pair. He then has another turn and proceeds to turn up two more cards in the hope of finding a pair. As soon as he turns up two cards that are not a pair, he must turn them face down again in the same place, and it now becomes the turn of the next player.

Each player proceeds in the same way, until all the cards have been captured. At that time, the player who has captured the largest number of cards wins the game.

SKILFUL PLAY: The trick is to remember the cards that have been turned up and exactly whereabouts on the table those cards are. For example, suppose the first player turns up a King and a 10. He must turn those cards face down, and you do your very best to remember exactly where that King is and where that 10 is. If it is now your turn, you try to turn up a card in an entirely different part of the table, hoping to find another King or another 10. If you find another King, you can go right to the first King like a homing pigeon and then you will have a pair of Kings. If you find another 10, you can go right to the first 10 and thus have a pair of 10s.

If you try to remember too many cards, you will forget them all. It is much better to begin by trying to remember only two or three cards. When you find that you can do that easily, try remembering four cards. In this way you can gradually increase your skill until you can accurately remember the whereabouts of seven or eight cards at a time. This should be enough to win almost any game.

TOSSING CARDS INTO A HAT

NUMBER OF PLAYERS: Any number, but the game is best for two or three.

THE DEAL: Give each player an equal number of cards from an old deck. If you have more than three players, take two old decks and divide them equally among the players.

OBJECT: to toss the largest number of cards into a hat.

THE PLAY: Take an old felt hat (be sure to get Father's permission before using his hat) and place it on a clean piece of newspaper on the floor at the other end of the room, with the crown down and the brim up. Standing the whole length of the room away from the hat, each player in turn flips one card towards the hat with the object of landing the card inside the hat.

Each player keeps track of the cards he has landed inside the hat. If a card lands on the brim, it counts as only half a point. If a card on the brim of the hat is knocked in by any player, it counts a full point for the player who originally threw it.

SKILFUL PLAY: The trick is to hold the card between thumb and forefinger with the wrist bent inwards towards the body. If you then straighten out the wrist suddenly with a flick and release the card at the same time, you can make it sail all the way across a very long room and you can control it pretty well.

Although strength isn't important in this game, small children may have trouble in getting the knack. As a handicap, they should be allowed to stand several paces closer to the hat.

SPECIAL ADVICE: Be sure to place the hat near a blank wall, and far away from a piano, or a sofa, or any other heavy piece of furniture. Cards that land under a piano are very hard to recover.

TREASURE HUNT

For this game you need two decks of cards, some preparation, two or three rooms with nothing breakable in them, and almost any number of young children.

You begin by hiding some of the cards from one deck in the rooms that you devote to the game. This must be done before the children arrive for the game.

Be sure to hide as many red cards as black, and be sure also to take out from the second deck cards that match the ones you have hidden. A hidden card should be discoverable without damage. For example, if you hide a card in a bookcase, it should be sticking out in some way and not hidden inside any book. Every hidden card should be well within the reach of even the youngest child. It is perfectly fair to put a card under the pedals of a piano, but not on top of the piano, where a small child would be unable to see it.

When the children arrive, appoint two captains and let them choose sides. One team will find red cards (hearts and diamonds), and the other team will find black cards (spades and clubs).

Give each child a card from the second deck and explain that he is to find a duplicate of it, hidden somewhere in a particular room or in two or three rooms, depending on how much space you have for the game. As soon as a child finds the card he is looking for, he is to bring it back to you and get another card to look for. The team that finds all of its hidden cards first, wins.

Be sure to explain that it isn't necessary to move anything in order to find the cards. Mention, also, that anybody who finds a card that he isn't looking for should replace that card in exactly the same spot and tell no one about it. Somebody else will be looking for it, or he himself may be looking for it later on.

This is a good game to play in somebody else's house.
(See also *Sequence*, p 34; *Snip, Snap, Snorem*, p 40; *Stealing Bundles*, p 82.)

2. The War Family...

Most games of the *War* family call on the players to keep their eyes open and their brains sharp, but they don't require great skill in the play of the cards. The skilful players usually win, but even the youngest player has a very good chance.

SLAPJACK

Slapjack is one of the jolliest games that can be played with a deck of cards. It is one of the very first games that my grandfather taught me, and he didn't complain when I won from him regularly.

NUMBER OF PLAYERS: Two to eight. The game is best for three or four players. Each player is a lone wolf, since there are no partnerships.

THE DEAL: One at a time to each player until all the cards have been dealt out. It doesn't matter if they don't come out even. Each player straightens out his cards into a neat pile face down in front of him without looking at any cards.

OBJECT: To win all of the cards.

THE PLAY: The player at the dealer's left begins the play by lifting the top card of his pile and dropping it *face up* in the middle of the table. The next player (at the left of the first player) does likewise – that is, he lifts the top card of *his* pile and drops it face up in the middle of the table, on top of the card that is already there. The play continues in this way, each player in turn lifting the top card of his pile and dropping it face up in the middle of the table.

As soon as any player turns up a Jack, the fun begins. The first player to slap that Jack wins the entire pile of cards in the middle of the table! If more than one player slaps at the Jack, the one whose hand is at the bottom wins the pile.

This means that the winning player has to keep his eyes open and has to be pretty quick to get his hand down on a Jack. Sometimes your hand is pretty red when you are so quick that another player slaps your hand instead of the Jack, but it's all in fun, and grown-ups are always careful not to play too roughly.

I used to beat my grandfather all the time because he would lift his hand high in the air before bringing it down on a Jack, while I would swoop in sideways and could generally snatch the Jack away before his hand even hit the table. That poor table used to suffer, but Grandpa never seemed to learn!

Whenever you win any cards, you must put them face down underneath the cards you already have.

The play goes on until one player has won all of the cards. As soon as a player has lost his last card, he may watch for the next Jack and try to slap it in order to get a new pile for himself. If he fails to get that next pile, he is out of the game. Sooner or later, all of the players except one are 'knocked out' in this way, and the cards all come to one player. He is the winner.

FALSE SLAPS: A player who slaps at a card that is *not* a Jack must give the top card of his pile to the owner of the card that he slapped. If the false slapper has no cards to pay the penalty, he is out.

How to Turn Cards: At your turn to play you must lift the top card of your pile and turn it *away* from you as you drop it face up in the middle of the table. This is to make sure that you don't see the card before the other players do. Also, you must make sure that you let the card go as you drop it on the table.

Naturally, you don't want the other players to have a big advantage, so you must turn the card over very quickly. Then you will see it just about as soon as they do.

Most players use the same hand for turning the cards and for slapping at Jacks. It's a more exciting game, however, if you follow the rule that the hand used for slapping must not be the same as the hand used for turning the cards.

Some players use the right hand to turn over the card with a quick motion, and they swoop down on the Jack with the left hand. Other experts, since they are much swifter at swooping with the right hand, turn the card over with the left hand. You may have to try it both ways to see which is better for you.

The important thing to remember is that it's better to be a swift swooper than a slow slapper.

SNAP

NUMBER OF PLAYERS: Three to eight. The game is best for four or five players.

THE DEAL: Any player deals, one card at a time, until all the cards have been dealt out. It doesn't matter if they don't come out even.

OBJECT: To win all of the cards.

THE PLAY: As in *Slapjack*, each player turns up one card at a time at his turn to play. The card must be turned away from the player and dropped on the table, except that each player starts a pile in front of himself for his turned-up cards. For example, in the game for four players, after each player has had a turn, there will be four piles of face-up cards and four packs of face-down cards.

When a player turns up a card that matches a face-up card on any other pile, the first player to say 'Snap!' wins both piles and puts them face down under his own pack.

A player who says 'Snap!' at the wrong time, when the turned-up card does not match one of the other piles, must give the top card of his pile to the player who just turned up his card.

As in *Slapjack*, a player who runs out of cards may stay in for the first 'Snap!' in the hope of getting a new pile. If he does not win the first 'Snap', he is out. A player who cries a false 'Snap' is out if he has no cards to pay the penalty.

SKILFUL PLAY: You have to keep looking around to make sure you know which cards are on top of the piles, since they keep changing as the game goes on. You must be ready at all times to shout 'Snap!' very quickly. If two or more players begin the word at the same time, the player who ends the word first, wins. If you're a slow speaker, this is no game for you.

My grandmother used to play this game with me. She preferred it to *Slapjack* – which can become rough – when one of the players was a girl. We had to make a special rule once because little Lisa said 'Snap!' every time a card was turned. She had to pay a penalty card most of the time, but this was more than offset because she won every single pile.

Grandma said this wasn't fair, so we adopted the rule that after three false 'Snaps' a player was out.

WAR

NUMBER OF PLAYERS: Two.

THE DEAL: Count out twenty-six cards for each player.

OBJECT: To win all of the cards.

THE PLAY: Each player puts his stack of cards face down in front of him and turns up the top card at the same time. These top cards start a new pile in front of the player. The player who has the higher of the two turned-up cards wins both of them and puts them face down at the bottom of his own stack. The King is the highest card, and the Ace is the lowest. The full rank of the cards is:

$$K, Q, J, 10, 9, 8, 7, 6, 5, 4, 3, 2, A$$

If the two turned-up cards are of the same rank, the players have a 'war'. Each turns one card face down and then one card face up. The higher of the two new face-up cards takes both piles (a total of six cards).

If the newly turned-up cards again match, there is double war. Each player once again turns one card face down and one card face up, and the higher of these two new face cards wins the entire pile of ten cards.

The game continues in this way until one player has all of the cards.

This is a good game to play when you have a lot of time and nowhere to go. I used to play it with my brothers when one of us was getting over an illness. It's just the sort of game to play at such a time, when you don't feel like thinking very hard or moving very quickly.

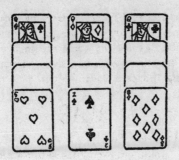

WAR FOR THREE

When three players want to play *War*, take any card out of the deck and give seventeen cards to each. For the most part, the play is the same as in two-handed *War*.

When two cards turned up are the same, all three players join in the war by turning one card face down and one card face up. If two of the new turned-up cards are the same, all three players must once more turn one card down and one card face up. As usual, the highest card wins all cards that are used in the war.

If all three turned-up cards are the same, the players must engage in double war. Each player turns two cards face down and then one card face up. If the result is a tie, all three players engage in single war.

BEAT YOUR NEIGHBOUR
OUT OF DOORS
(also called BEGGAR MY NEIGHBOUR and STRIP JACK NAKED)

NUMBER OF PLAYERS: TWO.

THE DEAL: Give each player half of the deck.

OBJECT: To win all of the cards.

THE PLAY: The non-dealer puts a card face up in the middle of the table. If it is an ordinary spot card (from the deuce up to the 10), the dealer covers it with a card from the top of his pile. This process continues, each playing one card in turn on top of the pile, until one of the players puts down an Ace, King, Queen, or a Jack.

The moment an Ace or a picture card appears, the other player must pay out the proper number of cards, one at a time, face up:

> For an Ace, four cards
> For a King, three cards
> For a Queen, two cards
> For a Jack, one card

If all the cards put down for payment prove to be spot cards, the owner of the Ace or picture card takes up the entire pile and puts it at the bottom of his stack. This is the way the cards are won, and the object of the game is to win all the cards.

If you turn up an Ace or picture card while you are paying out to your opponent, the payment stops and he must now pay you for the card that you have put down. This process continues, since either player may turn up an Ace or picture card while he is making a payment. Eventually, however, a player turns up only spot cards in payment, and then the entire pile is lost.

ANIMALS

NUMBER OF PLAYERS: Three or more. The best game is for five or six players.

THE DEAL: One card at a time until the entire deck has been dealt out. It makes no difference if the cards don't come out even.

OBJECT: To win all of the cards.

THE PLAY: Each player takes the name of an animal, such as pig, kangaroo, rhinoceros, hippopotamus.

When everybody fully understands which player represents which animal, the play begins. The player at the dealer's left turns up a card and then each player in turn turns up a card. As in *Snap*, the action takes place when a card that has just been turned up matches some other card that is face up on somebody's pile.

The players who own the two matching cards must each call out the animal that the *other* represents. The one who says the other's animal name three times first, wins both piles.

For example, suppose three boys have adopted the names, Goat, Pig, and Elephant. The first turns up a Queen, the next turns up a 10, and the third turns up a Queen. The first and the third go into action, but the second must keep silent. The first boy shouts 'Elephant, Elephant, Elephant!' and the third boy shouts 'Goat, Goat, Goat!' Both piles are won by the boy who finishes first.

Play continues in this way, until one player has all of the cards.

SKILFUL PLAY: When some other player is about to turn up a card, make sure that you have firmly fixed in your mind the card that is at the top of your turned-up pile. Then you will be ready to call out the other person's animal if he matches your card.

When it is your own turn to turn up a card, make sure that

you have looked at each of the other turned-up cards so that you can instantly spot if you match one of them. Nine-tenths of the skill in this game consists in being alert.

As you may have noticed, it takes longer to say 'Elephant, Elephant, Elephant!' than it does to say 'Goat, Goat, Goat!' For this reason, it always pays to give yourself a long animal name rather than a short animal name. The longer it takes an opponent to say your animal name three times, the better for you.

Good names to use in this game are: hippopotamus, rhinoceros, elephant, mountain lion, boa constrictor, and so forth. One boy, after reading about some of the ancient skeletons that had been dug up, tried to call himself *Pithecanthropus erectus*, but we didn't let him get away with it.

FARMYARD

This is the same game as *Animals*, except that the players take farmyard animals and go by the noises made by these animals instead of by the names of the animals themselves. For example, if the first player takes Cow, he is called 'Moo-Moo-Moo' rather than 'Cow, Cow, Cow'. Similarly, a player who took the name of Duck would be called 'Quack-Quack-Quack' and a player who took Cat would be called 'Meow-Meow-Meow', and so on.

I DOUBT IT!

I DOUBT IT (or CHEAT)

NUMBER OF PLAYERS: Three or more.

CARDS: Use a single deck for three or four players. Shuffle two decks together for five or more players.

THE DEAL: Two or three cards at a time so that each player gets an equal number of cards. When only a few cards are left, deal one at a time as far as the cards will go.

OBJECT: To get rid of all of your cards.

THE PLAY: The player at dealer's left puts from one to four cards face down in the centre of the table, and announces that he is putting down that number of Aces. The next player puts down one to four cards and announces that he is putting down that number of deuces. The next player in turn does the same thing, stating that he is putting down that number of 3s. The play proceeds in this way, in the sequence – Ace, deuce, 3, 4, 5, 6, 7, 8, 9, 10, Jack, Queen, King.

When any player puts down cards and makes his announcement, any other player may say 'I doubt it'. The doubted cards must immediately be turned face up. If the statement was true, the doubter must take the entire centre pile into his hand. If the statement was false the player who made the false statement must take the centre pile.

When the players are using two packs shuffled together, a player may put down any number of cards from one to eight.

When a player puts his last cards down on the table, some other player must naturally say 'I doubt it', since otherwise the game ends automatically. If the statement turns out to be true, the player wins the game.

A player who has no cards at all of the kind that he is supposed to put down is not allowed to skip his turn. He must put down one or more cards anyway, and must try to get away with his untruthful announcement. If somebody doubts his claim, he will have to pick up the centre pile.

If two or more participants say 'I doubt it' at the same time, the one nearest the player's left wins the tie. That is, he picks up the centre pile if the statement turns out to be true after all.

THREE-CARD I DOUBT IT

Deal the cards out equally as far as they will go, and put any remaining cards face down in the middle of the table. Each player in turn puts down exactly three cards. Instead of starting with Aces automatically, the first player may choose any denomination at all. For example, he may say 'Three 9s'. The next player must say 'Three 10s', and so on. When a player has only one or two cards left, he must draw enough cards from those put face down in the middle of the table to make up a total of three.

3. The Authors Family . . .

In all of these games the object is to *match* cards in pairs or sets of four of a kind. A good memory will help you in some of the games, but you can have a hilarious time even if you can hardly remember your own name!

GO FISH

NUMBER OF PLAYERS: Two to five.

THE DEAL: If only two play, deal seven cards to each; if four or five play, deal five cards to each. The rest of the pack is put face down on the table, forming the stock.

OBJECT: To form more 'books' than any other player. A book is four of a kind, such as four Kings, or four Queens, etc.

THE PLAY: The player at the dealer's left begins by saying to some other player, '(Jane), give me your 9s'. He must mention the name of the player he is speaking to, and he must mention the exact rank that he wants (Aces, Kings, Queens, etc), and he must have at least one card of the rank that he is asking for.

The player who is addressed must hand over all the cards he has in the named rank, but if he has none, he says 'Go fish!'

When told to 'go fish', a player must draw the top card of the stock. The turn to ask then passes to the player at his left.

If a player succeeds in getting some cards when he asks for them, he keeps his turn and may ask again. He may ask the same player or some different player, and he may ask for any rank in his new question. If a player who has been told to 'go fish' picks a card of the rank he has asked for, he shows this card immediately without putting it into his hand, and his turn continues. (In some very strict games, a player's turn continues in such a situation only if the card he fishes for completes a book for him.)

Upon getting the fourth card of a book, the player shows all four, places them on the table in front of him, and continues his turn.

If a player is left without cards, he may draw from the stock at his turn and ask for cards of the same rank as the card that he has drawn. After the stock has been used up, a player who has no cards is out of the game.

The game ends when all thirteen books have been assembled. The player with most books wins.

FISH FOR MINNOWS

This is a simpler way of playing *Go Fish*, and it is especially good for very young players. Deal out all the cards, not bothering if they don't happen to come out even. At his turn, a player asks for a rank, and the player who has been asked must hand one such card over if he has one. The object is to form pairs instead of books of four, and as soon as a player gets a pair, he puts them face down in front of him. The player who accumulates most pairs, wins the game.

AUTHORS

This game is very much like *Go Fish*, but can be played very seriously and with great skill.

All fifty-two cards are dealt out, even though they may not come out even. At his turn, a player asks for a single card by naming both its rank and its suit. For example, a player may say, 'Bill, give me the Jack of spades'. A player's turn continues if he gets the card asked for, but the turn passes to the left as soon as he asks for a card that the player doesn't hold.

SKILFUL PLAYING: When a player asks for cards and gets them but does not put down a completed book, you can tell that he has either two or three of that rank. For example, suppose John asks for Queens and gets one Queen from the player that he has addressed. John does not put down a book of Queens, but asks some new question and is told to 'go fish'. You now know that John held at least one Queen to give him the right to ask for Queens. He has received a Queen, which gives him a total of either two or three Queens.

In the same way, you know something about a player's hand, even when he asks for a card and gets nothing at all. For example, suppose Bill asks somebody for 9s and is told to 'go fish' at once. You know that Bill must have at least one 9 in his hand.

Little by little, you can build up information about the cards the other players must hold. If you know that another player has Queens, but you have no Queens yourself, the information does you no good. If you have a Queen yourself, however, you are then allowed to ask for Queens, and if you ask the right person because of the information you have, you may get an entire book and put it down in front of you.

OLD MAID

Number of Players: Two or more, each playing for himself.

The Deal: One card at a time to each player, as far as the cards will go. It doesn't matter if the cards don't come out even.

The Cards: Fifty-one cards, including only three of the four Queens. (Remove one Queen from the normal deck before beginning the game.)

Object: To avoid being 'stuck' with the last unpaired card.

The Play: Each player assorts his cards and puts aside, face down, all cards that he can pair – two by two. For example, he would put aside two Kings, two Queens, two Jacks, and so on. If he had three Queens, three Jacks, he would be allowed to put two of them aside, but the third Jack would stay in his hand.

After each player has discarded his paired cards, the dealer presents his cards, fanned out but face down, to the player at his left. The player at the left selects one card (blindly, since the hand is presented face down) and quickly examines it to see if it pairs some card still in his hand. If so, he discards the pair. In any case, this player now fans his hand out and presents it face down to the next player at the left.

This process continues, each player presenting his hand, fanned out and face down, to the player at his left, in turn. Eventually, every card will be paired except one of the three Queens. The player who is left with the odd Queen at the end of the hand is the 'Old Maid'.

Whenever a player's last card is taken, he drops out. He can no longer be the 'Old Maid'.

Skilful Playing: There is nothing to the playing of *Old Maid*, since it can be learned in about one minute and since there is nothing you can do to improve your chance of winning.

The player who is stuck with an odd Queen during the middle of the play usually looks worried and will squeal with delight if the player at his left selects the Queen. If you keep alert, you can usually tell which player at the table has an odd Queen as the play is still going on.

If you have an odd Queen in your hand, put it somewhere in the middle of your hand when you present it to the player at your left for a choice. Most players tend to pick a card from the middle rather than select an end card. Make use of this same principle to defend yourself if you think that the player at your right has the odd Queen when he presents his hand for you to make your choice. He will usually put the Queen in the middle somewhere, and you can usually avoid choosing it by taking one of the two end cards instead of a middle card.

It isn't bad to get an odd Queen towards the beginning of the play, for you will have many chances to get rid of it, and it will then probably stay in some other player's hand or move only part of the way around the table.

If you like to cause a little confusion, act worried when you don't really have a Queen in your hand. Another good idea is to squeal with delight when the player at your left picks some perfectly harmless card. This will make the other players in the game believe that he has taken an odd Queen from you. You, yourself, will usually know where the odd Queen really is, but the other players may be in considerable doubt.

4. The Stops Family . . .

The many games of the *Stops* family are all good fun, are all easily learned, and are all suitable for mixed groups of children and adults.

The simplest game of the family has no Stops at all, but it belongs in the family as a sort of great-grandfather of the other games. This parent form, called *Sequence*, is excellent for very young children.

SEQUENCE

NUMBER OF PLAYERS: Two to ten. Four or five players make the best game.

CARDS: Deal one at a time to each player until the deck is used up. It doesn't matter if some of the players are dealt more cards than the others.

OBJECT: To get rid of all of your cards.

THE PLAY: The player at the dealer's left puts down his lowest card in any suit he chooses to begin with. The rank of the cards is:

(Highest) Ace,King,Queen,Jack,10,9,8,7,6,5,4,3,2 (Lowest)

After the first card has been put down on the table, whoever

Best Card Games for Children

has the next highest card in the same suit must put it down. This process continues, until somebody finally plays the Ace of that suit.

For example, suppose that the first player's lowest spade is the 4. (This would be so if some other player had the 3 and the 2 of spades.) The first player puts down the 4 of spades, somebody else plays the 5 of spades, another player puts down both the 6 and the 7 of spades (it doesn't matter if the same person plays two or more cards in a row), and this process continues until somebody finally plays the Ace of spades.

When the Ace is reached, the one who plays it must begin a new suit. As before, the player who begins the suit must begin with his lowest card in that suit.

Sooner or later, one of the players will get rid of all of his cards. He wins the hand, and the other players lose 1 point for each card that they still have when the hand comes to an end. (A simpler method is to forget the scoring by points and just play to win the hand.)

SKILFUL PLAY: Practically no skill is required for this game. It is wise to begin with the deuce of some suit when it is your turn to begin a play. If you have no deuce, you should begin with a 3 — or the lowest card of any suit in your hand. If you don't follow this policy, you may eventually get stuck with a deuce or a 3 in your hand.

The great value of the game for very young children is that it is very easy to teach and that the children get practice in recognizing the numbers and in learning how the numbers follow each other in sequence. For especially young children, it is possible to remove the picture cards from the deck and use only the numbers from 1 to 10. In this case, of course, the Ace is the lowest card, and the 10 is the highest card of each suit.

NEWMARKET

NUMBER OF PLAYERS: Three to eight.

CARDS: The ordinary deck of fifty-two cards plus the four special cards (we'll come to them later) from another deck.

THE DEAL: The dealer gives one card at a time face down to each player, taking care to deal an extra hand as though there were one more player at the table. It doesn't matter if some hands have one more card than others.

PAY CARDS: The four pay cards taken from another deck, are the ♡ Ace, ♧ King, ◇ Queen, and ♤ Jack. These are placed face up in the middle of the table and remain there throughout the game. Before each deal, each player places 1 counter on each of the special cards. (The counters may be poker chips, matchsticks, toothpicks, dried beans, etc. All players should be given the same number of counters to begin a game.)

OBJECT: To win counters from the other players. This is done by getting rid of all of your cards or by playing a pay card and thus winning the counters that are on that special card in the middle of the table.

THE PLAY: The dealer looks at his own hand and announces whether or not he will auction off the extra hand. If the dealer wants the extra hand himself he puts his own hand aside, face down, and plays the extra hand in its place. If the dealer likes his own hand, he may auction off the extra hand to the player who bids the most counters for it. If two players make the same bid, the first one to speak counts. If both speak at the same time, the one who would play first going around to the left from the dealer wins the tie. If the dealer says he is going to sell the extra hand, he is not allowed to change his mind even if he is not satisfied with the results of the auction.

After the question of the extra hand is settled, the play begins. The player to the left of the dealer may begin with any suit, but must put down the lowest card of the suit he chooses to begin with. The player with the next higher card in the same suit continues, and the play proceeds as in *Sequence*. When any player puts down a card that is the same as one of the pay cards in the middle of the table, he collects all of the counters on that card. It is therefore an advantage to hold one of these pay cards in your hand.

If a player reaches the Ace of a suit, he must start with a new suit, but must play the lowest card he holds in whichever suit he chooses to continue with.

There is an important difference between this game and *Sequence*. You cannot always proceed up to the Ace of a suit, because you are sometimes stopped by the missing cards that are in the discarded hand. When no one is able to continue with a suit, the person who made the last play must begin again with a new suit, beginning (as always) with his lowest card in this new suit.

Sooner or later, some person plays the last card in his hand. He then collects from each other player at the rate of 1 counter for each card left in that player's hand.

SKILFUL PLAY: There is skill both in the auction and in the play.

A good hand contains one or more of the pay cards. Even if you have no pay cards, you may still have a good chance to play out quickly if your hand contains very few of the very low cards in any suit. It usually isn't hard to reach Queens, Kings and Aces, but it is often very hard to get rid of deuces and 3s.

As the dealer, you should be satisfied with your hand if you have one or more pay cards, or if you have a hand that contains practically none of the deuces or 3s. If you have a bad hand, containing no pay card and including two or more of the very low cards of the deck, you should exchange your hand for the extra hand instead of auctioning it off.

You follow the same principles if some other player is the dealer and offers to auction off the extra hand. The extra hand isn't worth a single counter to you if you already have a good hand. If you have a bad hand, however, you should be willing to bid up to 3 or 4 counters for the extra hand. If very few players are interested in bidding for the extra hand, you will probably get it for only 1 or 2 counters, but it won't be worth much. If the other players are satisfied with their hands, it is probably because they have pay cards in their hands, which means that there will be none left in the extra hand. However, there will be an advantage in exchanging your original hand for another hand because you will be the only player in the game who knows the cards in the discarded hand (that is, you will be the only player who knows these things if you have a good memory).

In the play of the cards it sometimes helps a great deal to know when a suit is going to be stopped. For example, suppose you know that the 9 of spades is in the dead hand. If you have the 8 of spades in your new hand, you can safely begin spades rather than some other suit. When you eventually play your 8 of spades, the suit will be stopped, and you will then be able to switch to some new suit. This gives you two chances to play, so it is always an advantage to be the one who switches to a new suit.

When it is up to you to start a new suit, it is usually a sound idea to begin a suit in which you have a pay card. This is your best chance to get the pay card out of your hand and thus collect the counters for playing it.

DOUBLE STOPS

This is the same game as *Newmarket*, except that the 10 and 9 of hearts are added to the layout in the centre of the table. In order to win the counters on the 10 and 9 of hearts, the same person must play both cards. This seldom happens, because sometimes the two cards are dealt to different players, and sometimes the cards are not reached. In such cases, the counters pile up so that they eventually make a rich haul for the player who wins them.

SPIN

This game is the same as *Newmarket* except that the player who holds the Ace of diamonds is allowed to play it in order to stop one sequence and start another. For example, suppose somebody else has started clubs and that the play has reached the 8 of clubs. You hold the 9 of clubs and the Ace of diamonds. You play both cards together, announcing 'Spin' as you do so. This stops the run in clubs, and allows you to begin the play in some other suit. You may, if you wish, then play a pay card if you have one, or you may begin with a low card in some new suit.

The player who has the Ace of diamonds is allowed to play it and call 'Spin' only at the time that he can make a normal play. In the example just given, for example, you would not be allowed to play the Ace of diamonds unless you could first make a normal play with your 9 of clubs.

SNIP, SNAP, SNOREM

NUMBER OF PLAYERS: Three or more players. The more the merrier.

THE DEAL: One at a time to each player, until the entire pack is used up. It doesn't matter if some players have more cards than the others.

OBJECT: To get rid of all of your cards.

THE PLAY: The player at dealer's left puts any card face up on the table. The next player (going around to the left) matches the play with the same card in a different suit, saying 'Snip'. The next player in turn (always going around to the left) continues to match the original play with the same card in a third suit, saying 'Snap'. The next player follows with the fourth card of the same kind, saying 'Snorem'. If a player is unable to follow with a matching card, he says 'Pass', and the turn to play passes to the next person on the left.

For example, the first player puts down a 6 of hearts. The next player to the left has no 6 and therefore must say 'Pass'. The next player has the 6 of diamonds and therefore puts it down, saying 'Snip'. The next player to the left has both of the remaining 6s and therefore puts them down one at a time, saying 'Snap' for the first of them, and 'Snorem' for the second.

The player who says 'Snorem', on putting down the fourth card of a kind, plays the first card of the next group of four. If he has more than one of a kind, he must put down as many as he has instead of holding out one of the cards for 'Snorem'. For example, if you have two Kings, you must put both of them down if you decide to play a King. It would not be proper to put down just one of the Kings and wait for the other two Kings to appear before showing your remaining King for a 'Snorem'.

The first player to get rid of his cards wins the game.

SKILFUL PLAY: There is no real skill in this game. It can be taught to even the youngest children, and they will be as good as the greatest *Snip, Snap, Snorem* expert after just a minute or so of practice.

THE EARL OF COVENTRY

This is the same as *Snip, Snap, Snorem* except that different words are used. The exact word depends on whether the player is young or grown-up.

Young children always use the same words when putting down their cards. For example, suppose a young player puts down a 5. He says, 'There's as good as 5 can be'. The next young player to put down a 5 can say, 'There's a 5 as good as he'. The next player says, 'There's the best 5 of all the three'. The fourth player would say triumphantly, 'And there's the Earl of Coventry!'

Grown-up players must make a different rhyming statement as they play their cards. For example, an adult who plays a 5 might say, 'Here's a 5 you can have from me', or 'The best 5 now on land or sea', 'The finest 5 in the land of the free', or any similar rhyming statement.

If a grown-up fails to make an acceptable rhymed statement when he plays his card, he is not allowed to begin a new play at his next turn at 'Snorem'. The turn to make the new play passes to the next young player at his left.

JIG

This is the same as *Snip, Snap, Snorem* or *The Earl of Coventry*, except that the players put down four cards in sequence instead of four of a kind.

For example, suppose that the player at the left of the dealer begins by putting down a 5. The next player must put down any 6 or must pass his turn. The next player must put down any 7 or must pass his turn. The play is completed by the next person who puts down any 8. The one who completes the play with the fourth card in sequence then begins the new series by putting down a card from his hand.

The game may be played by saying 'Snip, Snap, Snorem,' or by using rhyming statements as in the *Earl of Coventry*.

EIGHTS (or ROCKAWAY)

NUMBER OF PLAYERS: Two to eight. The game is best for two, three or four. In the four-handed game, the players who sit across the table from each other are partners.

THE DEAL: Seven cards to each player in the two-handed game; five cards to each player when more than two are playing.

The rest of the cards are put face down on the table as the stock, and the top card is turned face up to begin another pile.

THE PLAY: The player to the left of the dealer must match the card that has been turned up. That is, he must put down a card of the same suit or of the same rank.

For example, suppose that the card first turned up is the 9 of spades. The first player must put down another spade or another 9.

The newly-played card is placed on top of the turn-up card,

thus putting it up to the next player. It is up to the next player to match the new card either in suit or in rank.

The four 8s are wild. That is, you may play an 8 at any time, when it is your turn. When putting down an 8, you are allowed to call it any suit at all, as you please. For example, you might put down the 8 of hearts and say 'Spade'. This would call upon the next player to follow with a spade in order to match your card.

If you cannot play, you must draw cards from the top of the stock until you are able to play or until there are no more cards left in the stock. You are allowed to draw cards from the stock, at your turn, even if you are able to play without drawing. This is sometimes a good idea.

OBJECT: To get rid of all of your cards. The first player to get rid of all of his cards wins.

Sometimes a hand ends in a block with nobody able to play, and with no person having played out. The hand is then won by the player with the smallest number of cards. If two or more players tie for this honour the hand is declared a tie.

SKILFUL PLAY: The most important principle is not to play an 8 too quickly. If you waste an 8 when you are not really in trouble, you won't have it to save you when the going gets really tough.

The time that you really need an 8 to protect yourself is when you have been *run out of a suit.* For example, after several spades have been played, you may be unable to get another spade even if you draw every single card in the stock. If you are also unable to match the rank of the card that has been put down, you may be forced to pick up the entire stock before you can pass your turn. From here on, of course, it will be very hard for you to avoid a disastrous defeat. An 8 will save you from this kind of misfortune, since you can put it down in place of a spade, and you may be able to call a suit that embarrasses an opponent just as much as the spade embarrassed you.

If you're lucky, you won't have to play an 8 at the beginning, and you can save it to play out as your last card. If you're not quite as lucky as this, it is sensible to play the 8 as your next-to-last-card. With a little luck, you will then be able to play your last card when your next turn comes, thus winning the hand. To play an 8 with more than two cards in your hand is seldom wise. It is usually better to draw a few cards from the stock in order to find a playable card.

The best way to beat an opponent is to run him out of some suit. If you have several cards in one suit, chances are your opponent will be short in that suit. As often as you get the chance, you keep coming back to your long suit, pounding away at your opponent in this way until he is unable to match your card. If this is done often enough, your opponent will have to draw from the stock and may have to load himself up badly before he is able to play.

HOLLYWOOD EIGHTS

This is the same as the original game of *Eights*, except that a score is kept in points with pencil and paper. When a hand comes to an end, each loser counts up his cards as follows:

Each 8	50
Each King, Queen, Jack, or 10	10
Each Ace	1
Each other card	pip value

The winner of a hand is given credit on the score for the total of all points lost by all of the losers.

For example, suppose you have an 8, a 9, and a 7 when a hand ends. The 8 counts 50 points, the 9 counts 9, and the 7 counts 7. The total is 50+9+7, or 66 points.

In *Hollywood* scoring, three separate game scores are kept. The first time a player wins a hand, his score is credited to him in the first game score. The second time a player wins a hand, he gets credit for his victory both in the first game and also in the second game. He will thus have a larger score in his first game than in his second game score. The third time a player wins, his score is credited to him in all three games. He continues to get credit in all three games from then on.

Sometimes the game runs on until everybody feels like stopping. In this case, the three game scores are added whenever everybody wants to stop. The winner is the player with the biggest total for his three scores.

For example, suppose you win five hands in a row, with scores of 10, 25, 40, 20, and 28 points. Your score would look like this:

First Game		Second Game		Third Game	
	10		25		40
(+25)	35	(+40)	65	(+20)	60
(+40)	75	(+20)	85	(+28)	88
(+20)	95	(+28)	113		
(+28)	123				

A more popular method is to end a game as soon as any player's score reaches 100. When this happens in the first of the three games, the other two games continue. In the later hands, the score is entered on the second game and on the third game, but no further entry is made in the finished first game. Sooner or later, some player reaches a score of 100 in the second game, and this likewise comes to an end. Eventually, also, some player reaches a score of 100 in the third game, and then all three games have ended.

The winner is the player with the highest total score when all three game scores have been figured out and added up.

GO BOOM

NUMBER OF PLAYERS: Two or more.

THE DEAL: Seven cards to each player. The rest of the pack is put face down in the middle of the table, as the stock.

OBJECT: To get rid of all of your cards.

THE PLAY: The player at the left of the dealer puts any card down on the table. The next player must follow by matching the suit or the rank of the first card. Each player in turn after this must match the previous card in suit or in rank.

For example, suppose the first player puts down the Jack of diamonds. The next player may follow with any diamond or with another Jack. If the second player decides to follow with the Jack of clubs, the third player may then match with a club or with one of the two remaining Jacks.

When a player cannot match the previous card, he must draw cards from the stock until he is able to play. If a player uses up the stock without finding a playable card, he may say 'Pass', and his turn is then passed to the next player.

When everybody at the table has had the chance to play or say 'Pass', the cards are examined to see who has played highest. The cards rank as follows:

(Highest) Ace, King, Queen, Jack, 10,
9, 8, 7, 6, 5, 4, 3, 2 (Lowest)

If there is a tie for first place among cards of the same rank, the card that was first played is considered higher. The player who put down the highest card has the right to begin the next play.

The play continues in this way until somebody gets rid of all of his cards. That player wins the hand.

If none of the players is very young, a system of point scoring may be used. When a hand comes to an end, each loser counts the cards left in his hand as follows:

Each picture card	10
Each Ace	1
Each other card	pip value

The winner of the hand is credited with the total of all points lost by all losers.

SKILFUL PLAY: The strategy in *Go Boom* is much the same as in *Eights*. You try to run your opponent out of a suit in the hope that he will not be able to match your play with a card of the same suit or the same rank.

In the early stages of play, it is useful to play as high a card as possible in order to have the best chance to win the privilege of beginning the next play.

HOLLYWOOD GO BOOM

This is the same as *Go Boom*, except that the scoring is *Hollywood* style (three games at a time). As in *Hollywood Eights*, three game scores are kept for each player. The first time you win a hand, you get credit only in your first game score. The second time you win a hand, you get credit both in your first game score and in your second game score. After that, you get credit in all three game scores.

The first game ends when any player reaches a score of 100. Later hands are scored only in the second and third games. The second game ends when any player reaches a score of 100 in the second game. Thereafter, the scores are entered only in the third game score. When some player reaches a score of 100 in the third game, also, all of the scores are totalled to see who wins.

FAN-TAN
(also called CARD DOMINOES, SEVENS and PARLIAMENT)

NUMBER OF PLAYERS: Three to eight.

THE DEAL: One at a time until all the cards have been dealt. It doesn't matter if some players get more cards than others.

OBJECT: To get rid of all of your cards.

THE PLAY: Each player in turn, beginning with the player at the dealer's left, must play a card if possible. If he cannot play a card, he must put a counter into the middle of the table. (All players should be given the same number of counters to begin a game).

The possible plays are: Any 7; or any card in the same suit and in sequence with a card previously played.

For example, suppose that the player at the dealer's left put the 7 of spades down on the table. The next player may put down a new 7 or may play the 8 of spades, so that it covers half of the 7 of spades. The second player, instead, may play the 6 of spades so that it just half covers the 7 of spades. If the 8 of spades has been played, the next player has the right to put down the 9 of spades. Once the 9 of spades has been played, the next player has the right to put down the 10 of spades.

This process continues. At any turn, a player may put down a new 7 or may continue a sequence that builds up from a 7 to a King or down from a 7 to an Ace. The King is the highest card that may be played on a sequence and the Ace is the lowest card that may be played on a sequence.

The play continues until somebody gets rid of all of his cards. That player then collects all the counters in the middle of the table. In addition, each loser pays out one counter for each card left in his hand.

SKILFUL PLAY: It is usually easy to get rid of cards of middle size, such as 8s, 9s, 6s or 5s. It is usually hard to get rid of very low or very high cards, such as Aces, deuces, or Queens or Kings.

The way to play skilfully is to force the other players to build up to your high cards or down to your low cards. You can't always do this, but you can try.

If you have the 8 of spades, nobody can play the 9 of spades or any higher spade until you have first put down your 8. If a player who has high spades finds no chance to play them, he must play something else at his turn. This other play may be just what you need to reach your own very low cards or your own very high cards.

This shows you the general strategy. You play as much as possible in the suits that will lead you to your very high cards or to your very low cards. You wait as long as possible before playing in the suits in which you have only middle-size cards. If you have just a little luck, you will get rid of your very high cards and your very low cards fairly early. You will then be able to get rid of your middle-size cards in the last suit, catching the other players while they still have the very high cards and the very low cards in that suit.

LIBERTY FAN-TAN

This is the same game as *Fan-Tan*, except that it isn't necessary to begin a suit by playing the 7. Nobody can start a new suit until the previous suit has been finished.

The player to the left of the dealer begins by playing any card of any suit. The next player must follow with the next higher card in the same suit or must put 1 counter in the middle of the table. The third player must continue with the next card in sequence or must put 1 counter in the middle of the table. This process continues, building up past the King with the Ace, deuce, and so on, until all thirteen cards of the suit have been played. The one who plays the thirteenth card of the first suit may begin with any card in a new suit. Then the same process is continued with the second suit.

The player who first gets rid of all of his cards takes all the counters from the pool.

SKILFUL PLAY: Your chance of winning is best when you can determine which suit will be played last. If you have very few cards in this suit, you have an excellent chance to win all the counters since you will get rid of your few cards in that last suit while the other players still have cards of that suit left in their hands.

The time to choose the last suit does not take place after the third suit has been played since then there is no choice. The time for the choice occurs after the second suit has been played, since then two suits remain, and the player who chooses the third suit automatically fixes the other suit as the fourth suit to be played.

If you happen to end the second suit, by good luck, you will then begin the play of the third suit. Naturally, you should play your longer suit as your third suit, saving your shorter suit for last.

If the two suits are almost equal in length, it is sometimes wiser to play the shorter suit third and save the other suit for the last. The time to do this is when you have two cards in sequence in the shorter suit. If you start with the higher of these two cards, you will naturally finish the suit with the lower. For example, suppose you have ♠ K, 9, 8, 2. You notice that the 9, 8 are in sequence. Following the principle just mentioned, you begin the suit with ♠ 9. Other players follow with 10, J, and Q, allowing you to play the King. The Ace is played, you follow with ♠ 2, and others play on until your ♠ 8 completes the suit. Since you have completed the suit, it is up to you to start the next suit, and this is exactly what you foresaw.

The player who ends the first suit should use the same principle of starting the second suit with the higher card of two cards in sequence. This will allow him to end the second suit and thus make his own choice for the third suit.

FIVE OR NINE

This is the same as *Fan-Tan* except that the first player may put down a 5 or a 9 (instead of a 7). The card chosen by the first player sets the pattern for the rest of that hand. If he puts down a 5, for example, the other three suits must likewise be begun by 5s; and if the first player begins by putting down a 9, the other three suits must be begun by a 9.

Regardless of whether the play begins with a 5 or a 9, each suit builds up to a King as its top card and down to an Ace as its bottom card.

COMMIT

NUMBER OF PLAYERS: Four or more.

THE DEAL: Remove the 8 of diamonds from the deck of fifty-two. Deal the cards out one at a time, as far as they will go evenly. Put the remaining cards face down in the middle of the table to form stops.

OBJECT: To get rid of all of your cards.

THE PLAY: The player at the dealer's left may play any card to begin with. He and the other players can proceed to build up in sequence in the same suit.

For example, suppose that the first player begins with the 7 of clubs. Any player who has the 8 of clubs promptly puts it face up on the table. Then it is the turn of any player who has the 9 of clubs. This continues until the King of clubs is reached or until the sequence is stopped because the next card happens to be one of those face down in the middle of the table.

When the sequence is stopped for either of these reasons, the person who played last begins a new sequence with any card in his hand.

A player who holds the 9 of diamonds may play it if he has ended the previous sequence and it is therefore up to him to begin a new one. Another possibility of playing the 9 of diamonds occurs when all of the players have stopped with any sequence. When the 9 of diamonds is played, each player in rotation has the chance to continue the play either with the 10 of diamonds, thus continuing a diamond sequence, or with the sequence that was interrupted by the 9 of diamonds.

For example, suppose that somebody begins a sequence with the 3 of spades. The next player puts down the 4 of spades and then follows it with a 9 of diamonds. This gives a choice to the player at his left: he may continue with a 10 of diamonds or with the 5 of spades. If he has neither of these cards, the turn passes on to the left until somebody plays either the 10 of diamonds or the 5 of spades, thus showing which way the sequence will continue.

When you play the 9 of diamonds, you collect 2 counters from every player in the game. If somebody gets rid of all of his cards before you have played the 9 of diamonds, you must pay 2 counters to each other player in the game. (All players should be given the same number of counters to begin a game.)

When a player goes out (by playing all of his cards), the remaining players must show their hands. Any player who has a King must pay 1 counter to each of the other players in the game.

SKILFUL PLAY: As in the game of *Newmarket*, the best strategy is to begin with your lowest card in your longest suit.

It is helpful to remember the stops. At the beginning of a hand, the only stop you are sure of is the 8 of diamonds. It pays to begin with a low diamond if you have the 7 of diamonds in your hand, for then you will probably build up to that 7 and thus have the chance to begin the next sequence.

ROLLING STONE

NUMBER OF PLAYERS: Four to Six.

THE PACK: When four play, use the Ace, King, Queen, Jack, 10, 9, 8, 7 of each suit. If there is a fifth player, add the 6s and 5s. If there is a sixth player, add the 4s and 3s. There must be eight cards for each player.

THE DEAL: One card at a time until each player has eight cards. This uses up the pack.

OBJECT: To get rid of all of your cards.

THE PLAY: The player at the dealer's left begins by putting down any card he pleases. The others must follow suit if they can, playing high or low as they please.

If all follow suit, the player who put down the highest card leads again. In this case the cards that were played to this first trick are turned over and put aside.

Whenever a player cannot follow suit at his proper turn to play (the turn to play is always to the left), he must pick up all the cards previously played in that trick. This ends that trick, and the player who has picked up the cards begins the next trick by leading any card that he pleases.

This process continues, and in most games a player picks up the cards several times. Eventually one player will get rid of all of his cards, thus winning the hand.

For the purpose of winning a trick, the cards rank as follows:

(Highest) Ace, King, Queen, Jack, 10,
9, 8, 7, 6, 5, 4, 3, 2 (Lowest)

PLAY OR PAY

NUMBER OF PLAYERS: Three or more.

THE DEAL: One card at a time to each player, until all of the deck has been used up. It doesn't matter if some players get more cards than others.

OBJECT: To get rid of all of your cards.

THE PLAY: The player to the left of the dealer may put down any card from his hand. The player to his left must follow with the next highest card in the same suit or must put a counter into the middle of the table. (All players should be given the same number of counters to begin a game.) This process continues, with each player in turn obliged to continue the sequence or pay 1 counter into the middle of the table.

The cards in their proper sequence are: Ace, 2, 3, 4, 5, 6, 7, 8, 9, 10, Jack, Queen, King, Ace, 2, 3 (etc).

The player who puts down the thirteenth card of a suit makes the first play in a new suit.

The play continues until somebody wins by getting rid of all of his cards. Each player then puts 1 counter in the middle of the table for each card left in his hand. The winner takes all the counters out of the middle of the table.

SKILFUL PLAY: There is no skill in following suit; you either have the card or you don't. The only skill is in choosing the right card with which to begin a play.

If you have two cards in sequence in any suit, begin with the higher of these two cards. Eventually you will end that suit by playing the lower card of the sequence. This will give you the right to begin the next suit.

When possible, you try to get rid of your long suits first. If your shortest suit is saved for last, there is a fair chance that you will be the first player to get rid of all your cards.

5. Solitaire (Patience) Games . . .

Solitaire games are meant to be played when you are *solitary* or alone. They will help you pass the time pleasantly when you have to stay in bed or when you want to relax.

ACCORDION

(1 deck)

Deal the cards one at a time face up, in a row from left to right. Go slowly so that you can continually compare the last card dealt with its neighbours. Whenever this card matches its immediate neighbours at the left, or the card third to its left, you may move the new card over upon that which it matches. The matching may be in suit or in rank. Suppose that the first four cards you turn up are:

♠ J   ◇ 5   ♣ 8   ♠ 8

The ♠ 8 matches the ♣ 8 and also the ♠ Jack. You may move it over upon either card. Here, it is just a guess which play will turn out better. Later on, you will find that one play is better than another, when you have choice, for it opens additional plays. Keep watch for new plays made possible by consolidating piles. For example, suppose that you deal:

♡ 2   ♣ 5   ◇ Q   ♣ 2

you can move the ♣ 2 upon the ♡ 2. Then two clubs are adjacent, so you can move the ♣ 5 upon the ♣ 2.

Move the piles of cards as a whole, not just the top card. When a gap is left in the row because you have moved a pile away, shove all the piles leftward to close up the gap.

To WIN THE GAME you must get the whole deck into one pile. You will not succeed very often. You really are entitled to consider that you have won if you end with no more than five piles.

HIT OR MISS

(1 deck)

Deal the cards one at a time face up into a single wastepile. As you deal, count 'Ace, two, three . . .' and so on up to the 'King'. Whenever the card you deal is the same as the rank you call, that is a *hit*. Throw all the hit cards out of the deck. After you count 'King' start over again with 'Ace, two . . .' and so on. When you have dealt the entire deck, pick up the wastepile, turn it face down, and continue dealing. Also continue counting, from where you left off.

To WIN THE GAME you must hit every card in the deck. But you lose the game if you go through the deck twice in succession without a single hit.

EVEN UP

(1 deck)

Discard from the deck all face cards (Kings, Queens and Jacks). Shuffle the forty cards, then deal them one at a time face up in a row from left to right. Keep watch of the pairs of adjacent cards. Whenever such a pair is both odd (as two 7s) or both even (as two 8s) throw it out.

To WIN THE GAME you must throw out all forty cards in pairs.

KNOCKOUT

(1 deck)

Discard all 2s to 6s, leaving a deck of thirty-two cards. Shuffle it well, then deal three cards face up in a column at your left. If any is a club, throw it out to start a wastepile, then deal a new card to take its place. If the new card is a club, throw it out and deal another – and so on, until you have three non-clubs in the column. Then deal four more columns of three cards each, from left to right. From this array of fifteen cards, throw out all clubs into the wastepile. But do not fill the spaces so made in the four columns at right of the first.

Gather the remaining cards of the array and shuffle them well together with the cards left in the stock. In other words, shuffle all of the thirty-two cards except the discarded clubs. Deal a second time in the same way as the first, and having again thrown out all clubs, gather the remainder, shuffle and deal a third time.

To Win the Game you must discard all eight clubs in the three deals.

THE WISH

(1 deck)

I am reliably informed that if you win this game the first time you try it, you will get your wish. I cannot vouch for this, but that is what they say.

Use a deck of thirty-two cards, as in *Knockout*. Shuffle it well, then count off four cards at a time face down, then turn them face up. Be careful to keep the pile squared up so that you cannot discern the faces of any cards below the top. Deal the whole deck into piles of four cards in this way. Then lift off the top cards in pairs of the same kind – two 7s, two Queens, and so on. Keep going as long as you see any pairs.

To WIN THE GAME you must clear away all the piles in pairs.

CLOCK

(1 deck)

Shuffle the deck, then deal it into thirteen piles of four cards each, all face down. Arrange twelve of the piles in a circle, to represent the numbers on a clock dial. Put the thirteenth pile in the centre of the circle. Start play by picking up the top card of the 13-pile. Suppose it is a 5. Shove it face up under the 5-pile and pick up the top card of that pile. Suppose it is a Jack. Put it under the 11-pile, pick up the top of that pile – and so on.

Jacks represent 11, Queens, 12, and Kings, 13, other cards their pip value.

To WIN THE GAME you must get all the cards face up. The game is lost if you come to the fourth King before all the other cards have been moved face up to their proper hour piles.

KLONDIKE (also called PATIENCE)

(1 deck)

Deal a row of seven cards, the first (at left) face up and the others face down. These cards start your seven piles, which we will consider to be numbered from one to seven, left to right.

Next, deal a card face up on pile two and one face down on each of piles three to seven. Continue with a card face up on pile three and cards face down on piles four to seven. Continue in the same way, ending with one card face up on pile seven. Thus each pile has as many cards in it as its number; the top card of each pile is face up and all the others are face down. The rest of the cards are left on the side, face down, as the stock.

You may move the face-up cards to build them on each other. In building, you must alternate colours, red on black or black on red, and go down in sequence of rank. Thus the 4 of clubs may be moved upon the 5 of hearts or on the 5 of diamonds. Kings are highest, and may be moved only into space created by removing entire piles.

In building, keep the cards spread downward so that you can read them all. When two more more cards are built on each other, move all of them as a unit. For example, if you have a black 10 on a red Jack, you may move the two cards together on to a black Queen. Whenever you move the face-up cards away from a pile, turn up the top face-down card.

Aces are base cards. Whenever you have an Ace on a pile, or turn an Ace from the stock, put it in a base row above the piles. Build up on the Aces in suit and sequence: A, 2, 3, 4 . . . J, Q, K.

To WIN THE GAME you must get all four suits built up on the Aces.

After you have done all the building you can on the piles and Aces (if any), turn over the top card of the stock. (The stock is the undealt remainder of the deck.) Play this card on a pile or base if you can. If not, set it aside face up to start your wastepile. Continue turning up cards from the stock one by one, playing them when you can, and putting them on the wastepile when you can't. You may play off the top of the wastepile, if the next card turned alters the piles or bases so as to make such play possible.

You may go through the stock only once.

Alternatively you may turn over three cards at a time from the stock pile and then have the right to go through the stock pile as many times as you can, as in *Canfield* and *Beehive*, instead of once only.

SKILFUL PLAY: You must put Aces in the base row whenever they turn up, but you are not compelled to build on them when you can. It sometimes pays to keep cards on the piles, instead of moving them to bases, in order to help in building.

The important thing is to uncover all the face-down cards as quickly as possible. With a choice of plays (such as black 9s on two piles with a red 10 elsewhere), play off of the pile containing the most face-down cards.

You may prefer, however, to play so as to reach a single face-down card, since you will get a space if you can build with that card. It is helpful to get spaces when you can because Kings may be moved only into spaces. If you have no spaces, any Kings that you turn up will stay where they are and thus prevent you from reaching the face-down cards underneath them.

CANFIELD

(1 deck)

Count off thirteen cards face down, then put them on the table at your left, face up. Keep the pile squared up so that only the top card can be read. Deal one card face up on the table, above and to the right of the 13-pile. This card is your first base, and all other cards of the same rank will also be bases. Whenever you uncover any base card, move it up into a row beside the first.

Deal four cards in a row face up, to the right of the 13-pile. These cards start your building piles. Build as in *Klondike*, down in rank and alternating in colour. But your base cards are not necessarily Aces, as in *Klondike*. The rank of cards goes 'around the corner' – J, Q, K, A, 2, etc – and the circle is broken at the rank of the base cards. Suppose this is 5. Then 4s cannot be moved off the pile except to be built on the bases, while Kings may be built upon Aces.

To WIN THE GAME you must get the whole deck built upon the four base cards.

Whenever you get a space by clearing away one of the building piles, fill the space with the top card of the 13-pile. It is of course vital to dig into the 13-pile as quickly as possible. Build up in suit and sequence on your base cards, as in *Klondike*, remembering to 'go around the corner' when the bases are not Aces.

The undealt remainder of the deck is the stock. Turn up cards from the stock in batches of three, being careful not to mix their order. Lay each batch of three on a single wastepile. The top card of each batch may be played upon the piles or bases, and lower cards in the wastepile may be played off as soon as they are uncovered. Go through the whole stock by threes, playing what you can as you go. Then turn the waste-pile face down to form a *new* stock, and go through it by threes in the same way. You may thus run through the stock without limit, until you win the game or come to a standstill.

After your 13-pile is exhausted (all the cards having been played into spaces, upon the building piles, or on the bases), you may fill the space in the four piles by any available card you please. Don't be too hasty about filling such precious spaces. They are often needed to uncover a key card in your stock. Usually, fill a late space only when you have calculated that you will get it back again before reaching a blocked position.

POUNCE (or RACING DEMON)

This is a way of playing *Klondike* or *Canfield* as a round game, with any number of contestants up to seven or eight. The only limit is actually the number that can sit around the table and find elbow room.

Each player has his own deck. All the decks must have different backs, so that the cards can be sorted out later. Each player lays out his initial cards for *Klondike* or *Canfield* – whatever the game chosen. Everybody must be given time to complete the layout. Then at a given signal all begin to play.

Each plays the game in the usual way, building on his own piles, but all the base cards must be put in the centre and they become everybody's property. A player may build on anybody's base cards. The first to get rid of all his cards on to the bases wins the game.

If the play comes to a standstill before anybody has got rid of all his cards, the base piles are sorted out and the cards are returned to their owners. The one who got the most cards into the centre wins the game.

When the game is *Canfield*, a shorter game can be played: the one who first gets rid of his 13-pile wins. It doesn't matter where the cards go – into the centre or on his own building piles, so long as he is able to move them *somewhere*.

The game is very exciting, and rules should be enforced strictly to keep it from getting rough. A player may put cards on the centre piles with one hand only – his right hand, if he is right-handed. If several players try to put the same card on the same pile simultaneously, the one whose card is lowest wins the race and all the others must be taken back.

BEEHIVE

(1 deck)

This is essentially *Canfield* with simplified building.

Count off ten cards face down, then place them face up on the table at your left. This is the *beehive*. To right of the hive deal six cards face up, in any convenient arrangement, such as two rows of three. These cards are the *garden*.

The building is by rank; that is, a 9 goes on a 9, a Queen on a Queen, and so on. Build only on the garden, never on the hive. But remove the top card of the hive whenever you can, to put it on the garden. Garden cards or piles may be built together when they are of the same rank.

Whenever you make a space in the six places reserved for the garden, move the top card of the hive into the space, thus releasing the next card of the hive.

The undealt remainder of the deck is the stock. As in *Canfield*, go through the stock in batches of three cards at a time, being careful not to disturb the order of the cards. Put each batch face up on a single wastepile. You may play off the wastepile on to the garden. After exhausting the stock, pick up your wastepile without shuffling it, turn it over to form a new stock, and go through it again. You may continue going through the stock-wastepile without limit, until you win the game or are blocked.

Whenever you get all four cards of a rank together in the garden, throw out this pile, creating a space. After the beehive is exhausted, you may fill spaces from the wastepile.

To WIN THE GAME you must throw out the whole deck in fours of the same rank.

GAPS

(1 deck)

Deal out the whole deck face up, in four rows of thirteen cards each. Pick out the four Aces and discard them, thereby leaving *gaps* in the rows. Examine the card at the left of each gap. The next-higher card of the same suit may be moved into the gap. For example, if the 8 of diamonds is at the left of a gap, it may be filled by the 9 of diamonds. Moving the 9 of diamonds leaves a gap which you may then fill in the same way with the card next higher than the card at the left of the gap.

Whenever a gap is created at the left end of a row, fill it with any 2 you please.

To WIN THE GAME you must get all four suits in order, one on each row, from 2 to K going left to right.

When a King lies at the left of a gap, that gap is dead – you cannot fill it. Usually all four gaps become dead after some play. Then gather up all the cards except the Aces and the cards which are in proper sequence with a 2 at the left end of a row. Shuffle the cards well and deal them again so as to re-make the four rows of thirteen, but leave a gap in each row just to right of the cards that were not gathered up. That allows you to bring one additional card into its proper place on each row, to start you on a new series of plays.

When play again becomes blocked, gather and redeal the cards in the same way. You are allowed three deals in all.

Make the most of what choice you have in play. Choice often arises in the *order* of moving cards, and in the selection of a 2 to fill a left-end gap. It is surprising how often a good choice will open up many more plays than a poor choice.

PIRATE GOLD

(1 deck)

Deal ten cards face up on the table. You may place them in any convenient array, such as two rows of five each. Now, if any two of these cards are a pair (two Kings, two 5s, etc), cover each with another face-up card from the deck. Continue in the same way, dealing cards so as to cover all the pairs you see.

To Win the Game you must succeed in dealing out the whole deck.

The game comes out most of the time, but once in a while you will find yourself blocked, all ten cards in sight being of different ranks. In fact, when *I* played the game as a boy, I turned it around and considered that I won it only if a block arose and so I did not *have* to deal out the whole deck to cover all the pairs.

PYRAMID

(1 deck)

Deal twenty-eight cards face up in the form of a pyramid. Start with one card at the top, then a row of two below it with these cards overlapping the lower corners of the first. Continue with a row of three overlapping the row of two, and so on, ending with a row of seven at the bottom. Thus each card in the upper rows is overlapped by two cards in the row just below it.

At the beginning, only the seven cards in the bottom row are free to be moved away. As they are removed, cards in the upper row become free.

Whenever you see two free cards in the pyramid that total thirteen, you may remove them to a discard pile. Jack (counting 11) makes 13 with a 2, and Queen (counting 12) goes with an Ace (1). Kings count 13 and so may be removed singly. Begin the play by removing what cards you can from the pyramid.

The undealt remainder of the deck is the stock. Put this face down at your left, with the discard pile at your right. Turn up cards from the top of the stock one at a time. When you cannot use a turned card immediately, put it face up in a wastepile between the stock and discard pile. You may play off the top of the wastepile, just as you can play from the pyramid.

If a card turned from the stock makes 13 with a free card of the pyramid, or with the top card of the wastepile, you may remove such cards to the discard pile.

To WIN THE GAME you must get the whole deck into the discard pile – that is, match all the cards into 13s.

It is quite proper to keep the wastepile spread so that you can see all the cards in it. When you have choice of removing a card from the wastepile or the pyramid, try to calculate whether one play or the other will cause a block.

For example, suppose that three 7s are gone, two into the

discard and one into the wastepile. You turn up the fourth 7, and there happen to be free 6s on the wastepile and on the pyramid. If you take the 6 from the pyramid, you will be blocked, for the 7 needed to remove the 6 from the wastepile is buried below it. Therefore you must use the fourth 7 to play from the wastepile, hoping to be able to uncover the buried 7 to match with the 6 on the pyramid.

SIMPLE ADDITION

(1 deck)
Unless you are much luckier than I, you will not win *Pyramid* often. When you find yourself blocked for the umpteenth time, give it up and try *Simple Addition*. The principle is the same but you don't have to contend with all those buried cards in the pyramid.

Deal ten cards face up, in two rows of five. Remove two cards at a time that total 13 – Queen with Ace, Jack with 2, 10 with 3, and so on. Remove Kings alone. Fill the spaces by dealing additional cards from the deck.

To WIN THE GAME you must throw out the whole deck in 13s. You are bound to win if you succeed in dealing the entire deck.

LAZY BOY

(1 deck)

Shuffle the deck well. Turn it face down and take off three cards from the top, without disturbing their order. Put this batch of three face up on the table to start your wastepile. If the top card is an Ace or King, remove it to a row above the wastepile. Eventually you must get all the Aces and Kings in two rows above the wastepile, forming the bases. On the Aces, build cards of the same suit upward in sequence: A, 2, 3, 4, 5, 6, 7. On the Kings, build downward in the same suit: K, Q, J, 10, 9, 8.

Go through the entire deck, turning over batches of three cards at a time and putting the batches on the wastepile. Play off the top card of this pile when you can, either to put a base card (Ace or King) in place or to play on a base pile. The lower cards in the wastepile become available for play when they become uncovered.

Having exhausted the stock, pick up the wastepile, turn it over, and continue as before. Be careful not to shuffle or disarrange the cards in the wastepile. You may run through the stock without limit, until you have won the game or have been blocked.

To WIN THE GAME you must build the whole deck upon the base cards.

FOUR-LEAF CLOVER

(1 deck)

It is said that you will have good luck all day if you win this game.

Discard all four 10s from the deck – they are not used in the game. Shuffle the remaining forty-eight cards well. Then deal sixteen cards face up on the table, in four rows of four each.

Whenever you can, throw out from this array any two or more cards *of the same suit*, thus: (*a*) two or more spot cards that total 15, such as 9, 6 or 8, 4, 2, A (Ace counts 1); (*b*) three cards, the K, Q, J.

After throwing out a batch of cards, deal from the deck to fill the spaces left in the array of sixteen cards.

To WIN THE GAME you must throw out all forty-eight cards. Another way of saying it is that you must succeed in dealing the entire deck, for if you do, the final sixteen cards are bound to match up properly.

In making 15s, try to remove as many cards as possible, so as to bring in all the new cards you can. For example, remove A and 2 rather than the 3.

PERPETUAL MOTION

(1 deck)

Deal four cards face up in a row from left to right. If any are of the same rank (as 6s, Aces, Jacks, etc) move the others upon the one farthest left. Then deal four more cards from left to right on the four piles (counting a space as a pile if you have moved any of the first four cards). Play in the same way if you can, moving any two or more cards of the same rank upon the leftmost such card. All these moves must be one card (the top card) at a time; do not move a whole pile at a time. Continue dealing the deck four cards at a time on the previous piles, making what moves you can each time.

Having exhausted the deck, pick up the piles from right to left. That is, put pile four (at the right), still face up, on pile three (at its left); put these two together on pile two, and then the lot on pile one. Be careful not to disarrange the order of the cards. Then turn the whole pile face down, forming a new stock. Go through it again in the same way. You may similarly deal out the stock any number of times, until you finally win the game, or are blocked.

Whenever the four cards you deal at one time prove to be of the same rank, throw all four cards out, thus reducing the size of the stock.

To WIN THE GAME you must throw out the entire deck in batches of four of a rank.

You will see why the game is called *Perpetual Motion* the first time you play it. It really should be classed as an athletic game!

Solitaire Games

RUSSIAN BANK

This is a game for two players, based on the principles of solitaire.

CARDS: Each player has a regular deck of fifty-two. The two decks must have different backs.

THE LAYOUT: Each deals from his own deck a pile of twelve cards face down, at his right. This is his *reserve*. Above the reserve he deals a line of four cards, face up, extending towards his opponent. These eight cards (four from each player) start the building piles and they are common property. The undealt remainder of the deck is put face down on the owner's left; this is his stock.

BASES: All Aces are base cards. Whenever an Ace becomes available, it must at once be moved into the centre, between the building piles. The Aces are placed in two columns parallel to these piles, and they are collectively called the *centre*.

Cards may be built on the Aces, in the same suit and in upward sequence 2, 3 . . . J, Q, K.

BUILDING PILES: On these piles build downward and in alternate colours, as in *Klondike* and *Canfield*. The 4 of clubs, for example, may be moved upon the 5 of hearts or on the 5 of diamonds; the Jack of hearts upon any black Queen; and so on. A King cannot be built on another card in the building piles, but of course can go on a Queen of the same suit in the centre.

Cards must be moved one at a time from and to the building piles. (This is different from *Klondike* and *Canfield,* where you move the whole pile as a unit.)

THE PLAY: The turn to play alternates – you do not play simultaneously, as in *Pounce*.

At the very first turn of the play, the player must move into the centre, from the building piles, any Aces there, also any 2s, etc, that can be built on them. Having done so, he may turn the top card of his reserve face up. With exception of this very first turn, a player begins his turn with at least one card face up on his reserve. This point must be mentioned in explaining the rules.

A player must be very careful to observe the following rules in the *order* of play, else he may lose his turn.

RULES OF ORDER: An *available* card is one that is free to be moved elsewhere. The term covers: the top card of each building pile; the top card of the player's reserve; a card turned up from the player's stock but not yet put on his wastepile. The cards in the wastepile are *never* available. A card covered by another in a building pile is not available, though it becomes so if the covering card is moved away. The point of this remark is that a player cannot be charged with an error because he could have made a lower card available but did not do so.

1. Whenever an available card can be moved to the centre, this move must be made before any other. If the *reserve* card can be played to the centre, this play must be made ahead of a move from a building pile to the centre.

2. On clearing face-up cards off his reserve, the player must turn up the top face-down card *before making any other move*.

3. Available cards on building piles that can be played to the centre may be moved there in any order.

4. Having made all possible moves to the centre, the player is free to manipulate the building piles as he pleases to make additional cards available, create spaces, etc.

In the course of such manipulation, it is allowed to move any available card from a building pile into a space. A space is created whenever all of one building pile is removed. (Suppose that one pile comprises ♣ 9 and ◇ 8, there is a ♡ 10 on another pile, and that there is a space. By moving the ◇ 8 into the space, you can uncover the ♣ 9 and move it upon the ♡ 10. Then when you put the ◇ 8 back on the ♣ 9 you have *two* spaces instead of one. Look for such opportunities to create spaces, for they help you get rid of your own cards.)

5. A player must move the top card of his reserve – so long as it lasts – into a space, before he may play from his stock into spaces. He must fill all spaces in the building piles before turning up a card from his stock.

6. Having satisfied all of the foregoing rules, a player may turn up the top card of his stock. He must play it to the centre if possible; if not, he may put it on a building pile if possible. (See also *Loading*, below.) If he cannot find place for it anywhere, he must put it face up on his wastepile, and this act ends his turn. The turn continues so long as the player can find place for the cards he turns up from his stock.

The wastepile is a single pile placed between the player's reserve and stock. Notice that if you put a card on your wastepile your turn ends, even if there was actually a place to play it.

LOADING: You may build available cards not only upon the base cards (centre) and the building piles, but also upon your opponent's reserve card and his wastepile: this is called *loading* him. On his cards, you must build in suit and sequence, but the sequence may go up or down or both ways, as you please. For example, if his reserve card is ◇ J you may move an available ◇ 10 upon it. Should you then turn your own ◇ J from your stock, you can put it on the ◇ 10.

There is no use in loading your opponent from the building piles alone, for he can build the cards right back when his turn comes. But if you can cover such cards with one from your stock or reserve, splendid! – for you. You have got rid of some cards and have loaded him with some more to get rid of.

STOPPING: If a player violates any of the foregoing rules of order, his opponent may call 'Stop!' If the error is proved, the offender's turn ends.

In very strict play, you can be stopped if you so much as touch a card when you should move another one first. But you know how it is – we often touch cards merely intending to arrange them but forgetting to say 'I arrange'. A fairer rule is that a stop may not be called until a player has actually picked up a wrong card.

END OF PLAY: When a player's stock is exhausted, he must immediately turn his wastepile over to form a new stock. When his reserve is exhausted, he continues without a reserve, playing from his stock.

The first to get rid of his entire reserve and stock wins the game. He scores 30 points for winning, plus 2 points for each card left in his opponent's reserve and 1 point for each card in his stock and wastepile.

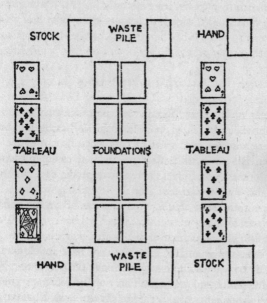

6. The Casino Family . . .

Games of the *Casino* family have been children's favourites for hundreds of years. They are especially recommended by educationalists, for they teach painlessly the first lessons in arithmetic. The word Casino is sometimes spelt – Cassino.

CASINO

NUMBER OF PLAYERS: Two to four. Best for two.

CARDS: The deck of 52 is used up in 6 deals. In the first deal, non-dealer receives two cards face down, and then two are put face up on the table, then dealer gives himself two face down. This whole process is repeated, giving each player and the table four cards each. For the remaining five deals, each receives four cards, two at a time, but no additional cards are given to the table.

THE PLAY: Beginning with non-dealer, each in turn must play one card from his hand, until all four of his cards are gone. If he can find no better use for it, the player simply lays his card face up on the table. This is called *trailing*. Whenever he can, though, he uses his card to capture cards from the table.

OBJECTS OF PLAY: To capture the most cards, to capture the most spades, to win Aces, the 10 of diamonds (Big Casino) and the 2 of spades (Little Casino).

PAIRING: You may win cards in various ways. The simplest is by pairing. You may capture a card on the table by another of the same rank from your hand – a 5 with a 5, a Jack with a Jack, and so on.

With a face card – Jack, Queen, or King – you may capture only one card, but with a card of lower rank you may take two or three of the same kind. If there are two 7s on the table and you have a 7 in your hand, take in all three 7s.

Each player keeps the cards he has captured in a single pile, face down.

BUILDING: All the lower cards, Ace to 10, may be captured by building. Ace counts 1, each other card its pip value. Cards on the table may be taken in by higher cards equal to their sum. For example, you may take a 5 and a 2 with a 7, an Ace and a 9 with a 10. You may at the same time take additional cards by pairing. Suppose that the cards on the table are 9, 8, 5, 4, Ace. You could take them all with a single 9 – since the 9 pairs, 8 and 1 make 9, and 5 and 4 make 9.

LEAVING A BUILD: Suppose that you have 8 and 3 in hand and there is a 5 on the table. You may put the 3 on the 5 and say 'Building 8'. Your intention is to capture the build with your 8 next turn. You cannot build and take in the same turn, because you are allowed to play only one card from your hand at a time.

If your opponent has an 8, he can capture your build himself. That is the risk of leaving a build. Yet the risk is usually worth taking, because in building you make it harder for him to capture the cards. He cannot take the 5 or 3 by pairing or by making a build of his own.

Of course, you must not leave a build unless you have in your hand a card that can take it. You are allowed to duplicate your build before taking it in. Suppose you have two 8s in hand. After building the 5 and 3, you could on your next turn simply put one 8 on the build, then take it with the other 8 on your third turn.

Or suppose after you build the 5 and 3, your opponent trails a 6, and you have a 2 in hand (besides the 8). You may put your 2 with the 6 on the 5, 3, and wait till next turn to take in the duplicated build.

An important rule is that when you have left a build on the table, you must attend to it at your next turn – take it in, or increase or duplicate it. You are not allowed to trail or to take in other cards instead.

INCREASING A BUILD: Suppose that your opponent has laid a 4 from his hand on a 5 on the table and called 'Building 9'. You have an Ace and a 10. You may add the Ace to his build and say 'Building 10'. You are allowed to increase a build of your own, in the same way. But there are two restrictions on increasing a build. First, you may increase only a *single* build, such as the 5, 4, not one that has been duplicated in any way, such as 5, 4, 9. Second, the card you use to increase it must come from your hand – you are not allowed to use a card from the table.

SCORING: After the last card of the sixth deal is played, any cards remaining on the table go to the player who was last to take in anything. Then each player looks through his captured cards and counts his score, as follows:

Cards, for winning 27 or more cards	3
Spades, for winning 7 or more spades	1
Big Casino, the 10 of diamonds	2
Little Casino, the 2 of spades	1
Aces, each counting 1, total	4
	—
	11

The one who reaches a total of 21 or more points first wins a game.

SPADE CASINO

This is *Casino* with a different count for spades. Instead of 1 for majority, the spades count: 2 for the Jack, 2 for Little Casino, 1 for each other spade. There are 24 points to be won, and the game is usually set at 61 and scored on a Cribbage board.

SWEEP CASINO

This is *Casino* with the additional rule that a player scores 1 point for each *sweep*. He earns this by capturing all the cards that are on the table at that time. To keep track of sweeps, turn the top card of your captured pile face up, for each sweep.

Winning the cards left on the table after the last deal, by being the last to make a capture, does not count as a sweep. But of course you could score a sweep by capturing all these cards in the regular way.

DRAW CASINO

Either *Royal* or the basic game can be played in draw style. To begin with, deal twelve cards as usual (four to each player and four on the table). Then place the rest of the deck face down in the middle of the table, forming the stock. After you play a card, draw the top card of the stock, thus keeping four cards in hand throughout the game. After the stock is exhausted, the hands are played out as usual.

The Casino Family

PIRATE CASINO

The 'pirate' feature is that you are allowed to make any play you please at a time when you have left a build on the table. You may take in other cards – even a build left by your opponent. You may even trail – and you do so automatically in the last deal, trying to make the last capture.

PARTNERSHIP CASINO

Four play, the two opposite being partners. The deck is used up in three deals. In the first, each player receives four cards and four are dealt face up on the table. For the other two deals, each receives four more cards, but no more are dealt to the table.

A player may duplicate a build left by his partner, without himself having a card that can take it. For example, if Tom builds 10, Nellie, his partner, may in turn put a 6 from the table and a 4 from her hand on the build, without having a 10 in hand. In all other respects the rules of *Casino* (basic or *Royal*) apply. Cards won by a partnership are pooled at the end of a play and counted in a common score.

STEALING BUNDLES

This is *Casino* much simplified for the very young. Deal as in *Casino*. Cards may be captured only by pairing, but any number of the same kind may be taken at a time. Captured cards must be kept in a pile face up, and you can capture your opponent's entire pile by matching its top card with a card from your hand. The object of play is simply to win and hold the majority of cards.

ROYAL CASINO

Children much prefer this colourful elaboration to the basic game. Since it is more complicated, young children should learn the basic game first, before attempting *Royal Casino*.

Face cards as well as lower cards may be captured two, three, or four at a turn. Furthermore, they can be used to capture builds; Jack counts 11, Queen 12, King 13. An Ace may be counted 1 or 14, as you please. Likewise, Big Casino in building may be used as 10 or 16, and Little Casino as 2 or 15. Sweeps are scored, as in *Sweep Casino*.

7. The Rummy Family . . .

Rummy is the most widely played of all card games. Many different forms of the game are played, but all have a very strong family resemblance. Once you have learned to play the basic game, you can pick up any variant form in a few minutes.

BASIC RUMMY

NUMBER OF PLAYERS: Two to six.

THE DEAL: Ten cards each, when only two play; seven cards each, when three or four play; six cards each, when five or six play. The rest of the cards are put face down in the middle of the table, forming the stock. The top card of the stock is turned face up in the middle of the table, thus starting the discard pile.

In a two-handed game, the winner of each hand deals the next hand. When more than two play, the turn to deal passes to the left exactly as the cards are dealt out.

OBJECT: To win points from your opponents. You usually keep track of these points with a pencil and paper score.

In order to win points, you must match up your cards. One way to match your cards is to get three or four of a kind. For example, you might have three Kings, or four 10s, and so on. A second way to match your cards is to get sequences – cards that are next to each other in rank and are in the same suit.

The rank of the cards in *Rummy* is:

(Highest) King, Queen, Jack, 10, 9, 8,
7, 6, 5, 4, 3, 2, Ace (Lowest)

A typical sequence is ♡ Jack, 10, 9. Another typical sequence is ♧ 4, 3, 2, Ace. You need at least three cards for a sequence.

THE PLAY: Each person at the table plays in turn, beginning with the player at the dealer's left. During your turn to play, you do three things: you draw, you meld (if you wish to do so), and you discard.

As you draw, you may pick up the top card of the stock or the top card of the discard pile. You add this card to your hand.

You meld by putting down on the table a group of matched cards. For example, you might put down three of a kind, or four of a kind, or a sequence. You might even put down two groups of matched cards if you are lucky enough to have them in your hand. You are not required to meld if you don't wish to do so.

After some other player has melded, you may add to his meld at your proper turn. For example, if some player has put down three Kings, you may add the fourth King at your turn to play. If some player has put down diamond 8, 7, 6 you may add diamond 10, 9, or diamond 9, or diamond 5, or diamond 5, 4, or any such card or groups of cards. You may add to a meld that has been put down previously by any player at the table (including yourself).

After you have drawn and melded (or after you have declined to meld), it is your turn to discard. You take any card from your hand and put it on top of the discard pile in the middle of the table. This act, called *discarding*, completes your play.

When a player, at his proper turn to play, manages to meld

The Rummy Family

all of his cards, he wins the game. He must begin his play with a draw, thus adding one card to his hand, and then he must meld either all of the cards in his hand or all but one. If he melds all but one card, that last card is his discard.

If no player has melded all of his cards (called *going out*) by the time the stock is used up, the next player may take either the top card of the discard pile or the top card of the new stock that has been formed by turning the discard pile over. In either case, play proceeds as before until somebody does go out.

SCORING: The winner of a hand scores points by counting up the hand of each of the other players in the game. Each loser counts his cards according to the following scale:

Picture cards	10 points each
Aces	1 point each
Other cards	pip value

A loser does not count cards that he has previously melded on the table but he does count any cards that remain in his hand, *whether or not these cards match.*

A player goes 'Rummy' when he melds all of his cards in one turn, without previously melding or adding to anybody else's meld. A player may go 'Rummy' by melding all of his cards after the draw, or he may meld all but one and then discard that last card. Whenever a player goes 'Rummy', he wins double the normal amount from each of the other players.

A pencil and paper score is kept, with a column for each player in the game. Whenever a player wins a hand, the amounts that he wins from the other players are put into his winning column. Some players agree on a stopping time when they play *Rummy*. The winner of a game is the player who has the highest score when the agreed time comes. Other players end a game when any player reaches a certain high total score, such as 500 points. The score for each player is added up at the end of each hand.

The Rummy Family

BLOCK RUMMY

This is the same as *Basic Rummy* except that the discard pile is never turned over to begin a stock again. When the stock has been used up, the next player has the right to take the top card of the discard pile. If he does not wish to take this top discard card, the hand ends immediately. This is called a block.

When a block occurs, each player shows his hand. The player with the lowest count wins the difference in count from each of the other players. If two or more players tie for the low count, they share the winning equally.

SKILFUL PLAY: In all games of the *Rummy* family, you try to build up your hand by keeping cards that match and by discarding cards that do not match. For example, if you drew the 10 of spades, you would tend to keep it if your hand contained one or more of the 10s, or if your hand contained the Jack of spades or the 9 of spades. In such cases, your 10 of spades would be a useful card. Even if it did not immediately give you a meld, it would bring you closer to a meld.

If you drew a card that did not match anything in your hand, you would either discard it immediately or would wait for a later chance to discard it.

If the player at your left picks a card from the discard pile, this draw gives you a clue to his hand. If, for example, he picks up the 9 of diamonds, you know that he must have other 9s or other diamonds in the neighbourhood of the 9. If convenient, you would avoid throwing another 9 or another diamond in the neighbourhood of the 9. This is called *playing defensively*. You would not bother with defensive play against anybody but the player at your left, since your discard would be covered by the time that any *other* player wanted to draw.

The advantage of melding is that you cannot lose the value of those cards even if some other player wins the hand. The advantage of holding a meld in your hand is that nobody can add to the meld while it is still in your hand. A second advantage is the possibility of going 'Rummy' all in one play.

It sometimes pays to hold up a meld, but most successful *Rummy* players make it a habit to put melds down fairly quickly. It is usually safe to hold up a meld for one or two turns, but after that, it becomes dangerous. If another player goes out before you have melded, you will lose for those matched cards just as though they were unmatched.

BOATHOUSE RUMMY

This is like *Basic Rummy* except that sequences go 'around the corner'. For example, you may meld K, A, 2 (all of the same suit) as a sequence. But you are not allowed to meld anything at all until you can meld your whole hand and go out. When you go out, you win points from every other player according to his *unmatched* cards, that is, the cards in his hand that he has not matched up in groups of three or four, or in sequences. There are two methods of scoring. One is to count 1 point for each unmatched card. The other is to count 11 for an unmatched Ace, 10 for a face card, and the pip value for all other cards.

One other peculiarity of *Boathouse Rummy* is in drawing. In beginning your turn, if you draw the top card of the discard pile, you may then draw a second card – from the discard pile or the stock, as you please. If you begin by drawing from the stock, however, you do not get a second card.

CONTRACT RUMMY
(LIVERPOOL RUMMY)

NUMBER OF PLAYERS: Three to eight.

CARDS: With three or four players, two decks of fifty-two plus one joker. With five or more players, three decks plus two jokers.

THE DEAL: Ten cards to each, except in Deal 7, when each receives twelve. The rest of the cards are put face down in the middle of the table, forming the stock. The top card of the stock is turned face up beside it, thus starting the discard pile.

OBJECT: To get rid of all the cards in your hand by melding them.

MELDS: The melds are as in *Basic Rummy: groups* of three or four cards of the same rank, such as Queens; *sequences* of three or more cards of the same suit, such as A, K, Q of diamonds.

THE CONTRACT: A game consists of seven deals. In each deal, a player's first meld must be a combination of two or three sets according to this schedule:

> Deal 1: two groups
> Deal 2: one group and one sequence
> Deal 3: two sequences
> Deal 4: three groups
> Deal 5: two groups and a sequence
> Deal 6: one group and two sequences
> Deal 7: three sequences

In melding the contract, Deals 1 to 6 inclusive, you may put down only three cards per set. If you have additional matching cards, you may put them down at any later turn. In Deal 7, however, you must meld all twelve cards at once, thus going out.

THE PLAY: As in *Basic Rummy*, a turn consists of a draw, melding (if you wish), and a discard. If you decide not to draw the top card of the discard pile, you must say so. Then any other player who wants it may take it. If two or more want it, the one nearest you in turn to the left is entitled to it. He has to pay for the privilege of taking the discard out of turn, by drawing the top card of the stock also. He must then wait his regular turn before melding or discarding. Then you resume your turn, drawing the top card of the stock.

Your first meld of any kind must be the *contract*. After that, you are not allowed to meld any new sets, but you may add matching cards to any sets on the table – yours and the other players'. A peculiarity of the game is that a sequence may be built to the Ace both ways, making a set of fourteen cards. (Of course, this rarely happens.)

WILD CARDS: The joker is wild. You may call it any card you please, to help you get rid of cards by melding. You must say exactly what card it represents. For example, if you put the joker down with the 7 of spades and the 7 of diamonds, you must say either '7 of hearts' or '7 of clubs'. The reason why you must specify is shown by the next rule. A player who holds the named card may, in his turn, put it down in place of the joker, thus getting the joker for his own use.

Many players like to have additional wild cards, to make it easier to form sets for the contract. Deuces are often used as wild, in which case 4, 3, A is considered a low sequence. A deuce cannot be captured, as can the joker. However, if a deuce is melded in a sequence, any player may put the natural card in its place and move the deuce to either end of the sequence.

ENDING PLAY: Play continues until somebody goes out. If the

stock is exhausted, the discard pile is turned over without shuffling to form a new stock.

SCORING: The player who goes out scores zero – which is good! Each other player scores the total of the cards left in his hand. Aces and wild cards count 15 each, face cards are 10, other cards count their pip value. The player with the *lowest* total score after Deal 7 wins the game.

KNOCK RUMMY

From two to six may play. Use one deck, giving each player ten cards when two play, seven cards when three or four play, five cards with five or six.

The play follows *Basic Rummy*, but there is no melding until somebody knocks. To knock means to lay down your whole hand face up, ending the play. You may knock in your turn, after drawing, but before discarding. You do not have to have a single meld to knock – but you had better have a conviction that you have the *low* hand.

When anybody knocks, all players lay down their hands, arranged in such melds as they have, with the *unmatched* cards separate. What counts is *the total of unmatched cards*.

If the knocker has lowest count, he wins the difference of counts from each other player. If somebody ties or beats him for low count, *that* player wins the difference from everybody else. When the knocker is beaten, he pays an extra penalty of 10 points. If the knocker lays down a *rum hand* – one with no unmatched card – he wins an extra 25 points from everybody, besides the count of unmatched cards held by the others.

The score is best kept with pencil and paper. Each item should be entered twice – *plus* for the winner and *minus* for the loser.

TUNK

Use one deck with two or three players; two decks with four or five. Each player receives seven cards. The rules of play follow *Basic Rummy*, and the object is to go out. Deuces are wild, and may be used in place of natural cards to form melds. To go out, you need not meld all your cards, but merely reduce the total of your unmatched cards to five or less. Before going out, you must give notice by saying 'Tunk' in your turn – and that is all you can do in that turn. A tunk takes the place of draw-meld-discard. Then the other players unload all that they can from their hands, and on your next turn you lay down your hand, ending the play. A player may at any time add cards to his own melds, or upon a tunker's melds after the tunk, but not on another player's.

The tunker scores zero, and the others are charged with the count of all cards left in their hands. When a player reaches 100, he is out of the game, and the others play on until there is only one survivor.

GIN RUMMY

Gin is one of the best and also one of the most popular of the *Rummy* games.

NUMBER OF PLAYERS: Two.

CARDS: A regular deck of fifty-two. The ranking is:

(Highest) K, Q, J, 10, 9, 8, 7, 6, 5, 4, 3, 2, A (Lowest)

THE DEAL: Each player receives ten cards dealt one at a time. The rest of the deck is placed face down in the middle of the table to form the stock. The top card of the stock is turned over beside it. This so-called *upcard* starts the discard pile.

THE PLAY: To begin his turn, a player must draw one card – the top of the stock or the top of the discard pile. Then he must discard one card face up on the discard pile.

Non-dealer plays first. If he wants the upcard, he may take it, but if he does not want it, he must say so without drawing. Then the dealer may take the upcard if he wishes. After he has taken or refused it, non-dealer continues with his turn. After that, the turn alternates and there are no further complications.

OBJECT OF PLAY: To reduce the count of one's unmatched cards.

A 'matched set' in *Gin*, is the same as a 'meld' in *Basic Rummy* – three or four cards of the same rank, or three or more cards in sequence in the same suit. For example, 6, 6, 6 is a matched set and so is Q, J, 10 of diamonds.

In *Gin*, Aces rank lowest, so that 3, 2, A is a sequence but A, K, Q is not. The point values are: Ace 1, face card 10, each other card, its pip value.

KNOCKING: There is no melding. Matched sets are kept in the hand, until some player brings matters to a halt by laying down all his ten cards. This act is called 'knocking'.

You are entitled to knock only if the total count of your

unmatched cards is 10 or less. You may knock only in your turn to play, after drawing and before discarding. You should make your final discard face down, as a matter of habit, thereby indicating your intention to knock. (If you should discard face up, intending then to lay down your hand, you could be stopped, for by rule the face-up discard ended your turn.)

The knocker must arrange his cards in matched sets with the unmatched cards to one side. It is customary to announce the total count of unmatched cards, as by saying 'I go down for five'. The opponent then exposes his hand, arranged by matched sets and unmatched cards. He is entitled to lay off cards on the knocker's sets, provided that it is not a *gin hand* – all ten cards matched. For example, if the knocker lays down three Jacks and the 9, 8, 7 of hearts (with four lown unmatched cards), the opponent can lay off the fourth Jack, the 10 or 6 of hearts, if he has any of these cards.

SCORING: Opponent of the knocker counts his remaining unmatched cards, after laying off what he can. If this count is higher than the knocker's, the knocker wins the difference. If the opponent has the same or lower count, he scores the difference (if any) plus 25 points for *undercutting* the knocker.

If the knocker lays down a gin hand, the opponent may not lay off any cards. The knocker wins the opponent's count, plus 25. This bonus of 25 for gin can be won only by a knocker. For example, suppose you 'play possum' with a gin hand until your opponent knocks with 1 or more. You win his count, plus 25 for undercut, but you don't get the bonus for a gin hand.

GAME: Keep score with pencil and paper. Enter the net result of a hand in the column under the winner's name, draw a line below the item, then write the total. The lines are important, to keep track of how many hands were won by each player.

The player who first reaches a total of 100 or more wins a game. He scores a bonus of 100 for winning, and an additional

100 for *shutout* (also called 'whitewash', 'skunk', 'Schneider', 'goose-egg', etc) if his opponent has not scored a single point. Then each player is credited with 25 points for each hand he has won. This is called the *line* or *box* score. The winner then carries forward the difference between his own grand total and opponent's grand total.

OKLAHOMA GIN RUMMY

This is simply *Gin* with the provision that the upcard fixes the maximum count with which you may knock. Thus, if a three-spot is turned for the upcard, it takes 3 or less to knock in that deal. If a 10 or face card is turned, the game is no different from regular *Gin*. Some players like to pep up the game with additional rules, such as: the hand counts double when the upcard is a spade.

AROUND-THE-CORNER GIN

In this game sequences may 'go around the corner' – thus K, A, 2 of clubs is a matched set. An unmatched Ace counts 15. A non-knocker is allowed to lay off cards even on a gin hand. The game is usually set at 125 points. In all other respects the regular *Gin* rules apply.

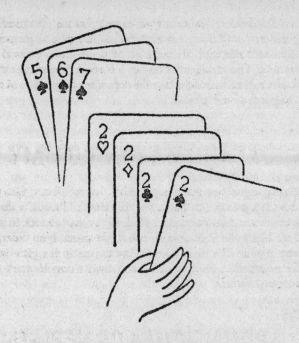

500 RUMMY (SEQUENCE RUMMY)

The chief feature of *500 Rummy* is that you score for melding as well as for going out.

NUMBER OF PLAYERS: Three to eight. When more than four play, they should use two decks of fifty-two shuffled together.

THE DEAL: Seven cards to each. The turn to deal passes to the left.

THE PLAY: As in *Basic Rummy*, a player may begin his turn by drawing the top card of the stock or the discard pile. But he has a third choice – he may draw *any* card of the discard pile, no matter how deeply it is buried, provided that he immediately melds this card. He must also pick up all the cards that covered it, and add them to his hand. He may proceed to meld all the cards he wishes to; his turn ends when he discards.

Discards are not stacked in a pile, as in most *Rummy* games, but are spread out in an overlapping fan so that all the cards can be seen. It is of course important not to mix up the order in which they lie. When you 'dig deep' into the discards, courtesy requires that you leave the cards on the table for a while, to give the other players a chance to see what you are getting, before you put them into your hand.

Melds are as in *Basic Rummy*. You may add cards to your own melds and also to those belonging to other players. Since all the cards you meld count for you, you should keep them in front of *yourself*, merely pointing out the melds to which they may be attached. For example, if somebody has melded 9, 8, 7 of clubs, you may lay down the 10 of clubs. Then later any player may lay down the Jack of clubs – still keeping possession of it.

Play ends when some player gets rid of all the cards from his hand. He may meld all his cards without making a final discard. If nobody goes out by the time the stock is exhausted, play continues so long as each in turn draws from the discard pile, but ends as soon as any player fails to do so.

SCORING: When play ends, each player counts up the difference between the cards he has melded and the cards left in his hand. This difference (which may be plus or minus) is added to his running total score, which is kept on paper.

The cards count as follows: Ace 15, unless it was melded in a low sequence (A, 2, 3), in which case it counts 1; face cards 10 each, other cards, their pip value.

The player who first wins 500 points wins the game.

SKILFUL PLAY: Much more is won by melding than by going out. You should try to meld as much as possible, and to meld high cards rather than low cards. For this purpose, you want to get as many cards into your hand as you can. The deeper you have to dig into the discard pile, the happier you are!

If you are dealt a low meld, such as three deuces, discard one of them at first opportunity. Then, after the discard pile has grown to ten or twelve cards, reclaim your deuce to meld it – and so get some booty! Just remember not to be greedy; if you wait too long, somebody else may take the pile, for you can be sure that the others will 'salt' the pile too, if they have the chance.

At the beginning of a game, try to avoid making it too easy for another player to take the discard pile. You may make it easy if you discard a card that pairs with another already in the pile, or that is in suit and sequence with one in the pile. Of course, there comes a time when you have no more safe discards. Then follow the principle of doing the least damage. Discard a card that may let another player take a *few* cards, rather than a great many.

As a rule, don't meld except when you have to in order to dig into the discard pile. Keeping a meld of high cards in your hand, especially Aces, puts the fellow who has the fourth Ace on the spot. If he discards it, he gives you a chance to pick up the pile; if he holds it, he may get stuck with it. If you meld your Aces, his troubles are over. If you are too lavish in melding, you may help another player to go out.

You must be quick to change policy, however, when the stock is nearly gone or when another player reduces his hand to only a few cards. Meld your high cards then, to be sure that they will count *for* you instead of against you.

8. Trump Games . . .

A trump suit is one which is given a special privilege: it ranks higher than all the other suits. For example, if spades are trumps, a spade will win any heart, club, or diamond. The deuce of spades can take the Ace of hearts, although the Ace of hearts can win any lower heart.

In some games, the trump suit is decided by turning up a card from the deck – its suit becomes trumps. In other games, the right to name the trump suit is decided by bidding. The right goes to the player who is willing to pay the highest price for it. A player bids what he is willing to pay. This may be a number of counters that he puts in a pool. Usually, each bidder names a number of points or tricks that the bidder hopes to win. The one who names the trump must win at least what he has bid, in order to advance his score. If he fails, points are taken away from him, or his opponents score (according to the particular game). Failing to make a bid goes by different names (in different games) – 'set', 'euchre', 'bate', and so on.

LINGER LONGER

A good game to start with in learning the trump games.

NUMBER OF PLAYERS: Four to six.

CARDS: Each receives as many cards as there are players in the game. For example, with five players, each receives five cards. The last card dealt, belonging to the dealer, is shown to all the players. It decides the trump suit for that hand. The rest of the deck is placed face down in the middle of the table, forming the stock.

THE PLAY: The player at left of the dealer makes the first lead. The cards are played out in tricks. A player must follow suit to the lead when able. Otherwise, he may lead or play what he pleases. A trick is won by the highest trump, or, if it contains no trump, by the highest card played of the suit led.

When a player wins a trick, he draws the top card of the stock. Nobody else draws. Thus some players get more cards than others. When a player is left without any cards, he drops out of the hand, and the others play on. The last one left, after all the others have had to drop out, wins the game. If two or more are down to one card each at the end, the winner of the last trick wins the game.

NAPOLEON (NAP)

NUMBER OF PLAYERS: Two to six. The more, the merrier.

CARDS: A regular deck of fifty-two. Ace ranks highest. Each player receives five cards, one at a time.

BIDDING: Player at left of the dealer has first turn to bid the number of tricks he will take if he is allowed to name the trump suit. Each has one turn, in which he may pass or may bid from one to five. A bid of five is called *nap*.

THE PLAY: The highest bidder names the trump suit and has the first lead. He must lead a trump for his first lead. The cards are played in tricks. A player must follow suit to the lead if he can. Otherwise, there is no restriction on what he may play or lead. A bid of nap with a predetermined suit takes precedence over a nap bid on any other suit.

The bidder tries to win the number of tricks he has named. All the other players combine forces against him. Play stops the moment the outcome is sure – success or defeat for the bidder.

SCORING: All the players get equal numbers of counters at the beginning of a game. When a bidder wins, he collects from each other player the same number of counters as his bid. If he is defeated, he pays this number to each. The bid of nap (all the tricks) is special. If it is made, the bidder collects 10 counters each, but if he fails he pays only 5 each.

LOO

NUMBER OF PLAYERS: Five to eight.

CARDS: A regular deck of fifty-two. Each player receives three cards, one at a time. An extra hand is dealt just to left of the dealer. This is the *widow*. The player at left of the widow, if he does not like his hand, may throw it away and take the widow instead. If he is satisfied with his hand, he must say so. Then each player in turn has a chance to take the widow, until somebody takes it or all refuse it.

THE PLAY (SINGLE POOL): After the matter of the widow is settled, the player at left of the dealer makes the opening lead. A player must always follow suit to the lead when he can, must *play higher* than any other card on the trick when he can, and when a plain suit is led of which he has none, must *trump* if he can.

The highest trump, or the highest card of the suit led, wins a trick. Ace is highest card.

The cards played are not thrown together in the middle of the table. Everybody keeps possession of his cards, placing them face up on the table in front of himself as he plays them.

TRUMPS: The play begins without any trump suit, and continues that way so long as everybody follows suit to every lead. When somebody fails to follow suit, play to the trick is finished, then the top card of the undealt remainder of the deck is turned over. This card decides the trump suit. The trick just played must be examined to see who won the trick, since a card that was merely 'discarded' may turn out to be a trump.

SCORING: To begin a game, all players receive equal numbers of counters. Each dealer must *ante* 3 counters to start a pool. When the pool contains no more than these 3, it is a *single*, and the play is as described above. After the play, the pool pays out 1 counter for each trick won. Every player who has won no trick must pay 3 counters into the next pool thus making it a *double* (or jackpot).

DOUBLE POOL: This is formed by dealer's ante plus payments for *loo* (not winning a trick in the previous hand). After the deal, the next card of the deck is turned, deciding the trump suit immediately. The players look at their hands and each in turn must say whether he will play or drop out. If all but the dealer drop out, he takes the pool. If only one player ahead of the dealer decides to play, the dealer is obliged to play, too. He may play for himself, in which case he cannot take the widow. Or he may play to 'defend the pool', in which case he must throw away his hand and take the widow.

The nearest active player at left of the dealer leads first. The other rules of play are the same as in a single pool.

The double pool pays out one-third of its contents for each trick won. A player who stayed in and won no trick must pay 3 counters to the next pool. When the dealer plays merely to 'defend the pool', he neither collects nor pays any counters; the pool settles with his opponent alone.

RAMS

This game is very similar to *Loo*.

NUMBER OF PLAYERS: Three to five.

CARDS: A deck of thirty-two. Discard all 2s and 6s from a regular deck of fifty-two. The cards in each suit rank:

(Highest) A, K, Q, J, 10, 9, 8, 7 (Lowest)

Each player receives five cards in batches of three and two. An extra hand or *widow* is dealt, as in *Loo*. The last card, belonging to the dealer, is exposed to determine the trump suit. Undealt cards are put aside until the next deal.

DECLARING: Beginning with the player at the left of the dealer, each in turn must declare whether he will play or will drop out. If he plays, he undertakes to win at least one trick. Any player in his turn may discard his hand and take the widow instead (if it has not been taken before him).

Any player may declare *rams*. This means that he will undertake to win *all* the tricks. He may make this declaration either before or after taking the widow, but must make it before the next player in turn has declared. In a rams, everybody must play; any who have dropped out must pick up their hands again. If the rams player has not taken the widow, each player who has not refused it or has not dropped out gets a chance to take it.

THE PLAY: A player who declares rams makes the opening lead. Otherwise, it is made by the player nearest dealer's left, among those who have decided to play.

A player must follow suit when he can, and must play higher than any previous card on the trick, when he can. If a plain suit is led, he must trump if able, even if the trick has already been trumped. A trick is won by the highest trump in it, or, if it contains no trump, by the highest card played of the suit led.

SCORING: Equal numbers of counters are distributed to all players at the beginning of a game. The dealer *antes* 5 counters into a pool. After the game gets under way, the pool also contains payments from the previous deal.

Each player who has stayed in takes 1 counter (or one-fifth of the counters) from the pool for each trick he wins. Each who wins no trick must pay 5 counters into the next pool.

In a rams, however, the settlement is different. If the rams player wins all the tricks, he wins the whole pool plus 5 counters from every other player. If he loses a single trick, the cards are at once thrown in; he must pay counters to double the pool and 5 counters to every other player.

If everybody ahead of the player at right of the dealer passes, this player must pay the dealer 5 counters if he wishes to drop. In this case, the pool remains undivided. If only one player other than the dealer decides to play, the dealer must play to defend the pool. In this case he is allowed to take the trump card and discard another face down.

SIXTY-SIX

NUMBER OF PLAYERS: Two, but variants for three and four are given below.

CARDS: A deck of twenty-four cards: A, K, Q, J, 10, 9 of each suit. (Discard all 2s to 8s from a regular deck.) Each player receives six cards, dealt three at a time. The rest of the deck is placed face down in the middle of the table, to form the stock. The top card of the stock is turned face up and placed partly underneath the stock. This card decides the trump suit.

RANK: The cards in each suit rank

(Highest) A, 10, K, Q, J, 9 (Lowest)

EARLY PLAY: The non-dealer leads first. The cards are played out in tricks. A trick is won by the higher trump or by the higher card of the suit led. The winner of a trick draws the top card of the stock, and his opponent draws the next card. Thus each hand is restored to six cards after each trick.

During this early play (before the stock is exhausted), you do not have to follow suit to the lead: you may play any card.

OBJECTS OF PLAY: To meld marriages, to win counting cards in tricks, and to win last trick.

MARRIAGES: A marriage is a King and a Queen of the same suit. In the trump suit, a marriage counts 40; in any other suit, 20. To score a marriage you must show it after winning a trick, then lead one of the two cards.

If non-dealer wants to lead a King or Queen from a marriage for the opening lead, he may show the marriage and do so. But he does not score the marriage until after he has won a trick.

TRUMP CARD: A player having the 9 of trumps may exchange it for the trump card (to get a higher trump). You may make this exchange only after winning a trick, before making the next lead.

CLOSING: At any turn to lead, a player may turn the trump card face down. This signifies that he closes, that is, stops any further drawing from the stock. The hands are played out as in *Later Play* (below), with the difference that marriages may still be melded.

LATER PLAY: After the stock is exhausted, the six cards in each hand are played out. At this time, a player must follow suit to the lead if he can.

COUNTING CARDS: Cards won in tricks are counted as follows:

Each Ace	11
Each ten	10
Each King	4
Each Queen	3
Each Jack	2
(No count for 9s)	
For winning last trick	10

SCORING: The player who first reaches a total of 66 or more wins a game.

Marriages are scored on paper whenever melded. Points taken in tricks are not entered on paper until a hand is finished, but an important feature is to keep mental track of these points as they are won. In your turn to play, you may claim that you have reached 66. Play stops at once and the cards are counted. If you are right, you score 1 game point – or 2 if your opponent has less than 33, or 3 if he has not even won a trick. If you are wrong, not having 66, your opponent scores 2 game points.

It is important to realize when you have won a game, and to claim it, because you may lose by playing out the hand. If you and your opponent both get more than 66, or if you tie at 65, neither wins. But the winner of the next hand gets 1 additional game point.

Usually, at least 1 game point is won by somebody each deal. The one who first scores 7 game points wins an overall game.

THREE-HAND SIXTY-SIX

The dealer gives cards to the other two but none to himself. They play regular two-hand *Sixty-Six*. The dealer scores the same number of game points as the winner of the deal. If both players get 66 or more, or tie at 65 (without a claim), they score nothing and dealer gets 1. But a player is not allowed to win the overall game (7 points) as dealer. If the usual scoring would put him up to 7 or over, his total becomes 6, and he must win the last point as an active player.

FOUR-HAND SIXTY-SIX

The players sitting opposite each other are partners. The deck is increased to thirty-two cards by adding the 8s and 7s. All the cards are dealt out, each player receiving eight. The last card is turned for trump, then taken in hand by the dealer.

There is no melding. At all times a player must follow suit to a lead, if he can, and also must if possible play higher than any card already played to the trick. When a plain suit is led and he has none, he must trump or overtrump if he can.

Every hand is played out. There is no advantage in claiming to have won. The winning side scores 1 game point for having taken 66 to 99, or 2 for 100 to 129, or 3 for every trick (130). If the sides tie at 65, 1 extra game point goes to the side winning the next hand.

Trump Games

9. The Whist Family . . .

Back in the 1890s the games editor of an English magazine received a letter to this effect:

'My son, aged nine, has seen his elders playing Whist and now wishes to learn the game. Can you recommend to me some simple game I can teach him, which will serve as an introduction to Whist?'

The editor replied, 'Yes, I can recommend such a game. The game is Whist.'

The fact is that the rules of *Whist* are simple and few. They can be learned in two minutes. *Whist* is just about the simplest of all card games to play *at*. What is not so easy is to play *Whist* well, for its extraordinary scope for skilful play lets the expert pull miles ahead of the beginner.

WHIST

NUMBER OF PLAYERS: Four in partnerships.

CARDS: Each receives thirteen cards, dealt one at a time. The last card of the deck, belonging to the dealer, is exposed to all the players. This card decides the trump suit for that hand.

RANK: In every suit the cards rank

(Highest) A, K, Q, J, 10, 9, 8, 7, 6, 5, 4, 3, 2 (Lowest)

THE PLAY: The player at left of the dealer makes the first lead. The hands are played out in tricks. A player must follow suit to the lead if he can. Otherwise he may play or lead as he pleases. A trick is won by the highest trump in it, or, if it contains no trump, by the highest card of the suit led. The winner of a trick makes the lead for the next trick.

One member of each partnership gathers together all the tricks won by his side. The tricks are not thrown together in a single pile, but are overlapped so that each batch of four cards remains separated from the others.

OBJECT OF PLAY: To win as many tricks as possible.

SCORING: The side that wins a majority of the tricks scores 1 point for each trick over six. These are called *odd tricks*.

In addition, points are scored for *honours*. The honours are the A, K, Q, and J of trumps. If two honours were dealt to each side, there is no score. If one side received three honours it scores 2; for four honours, the score is 4.

Remember that honours are scored by the side to which they are *dealt*, not won in play. Both sides may score in the same deal, one side winning a majority of tricks and the other side holding a majority of honours.

GAME: Points for odd tricks and honours are accumulated, and the side first reaching a total of 7 points wins a game.

DUMMY WHIST

This is an adaptation of the game to three players. Four hands are dealt as usual, the extra hand or 'dummy' being dealt opposite the dealer. The latter plays the dummy as well as his own hand against the two live opponents. Of course, dealer must be careful to play from his two hands in proper turn. He has a great advantage over his opponents, since he sees all twenty-six cards on his side. The fairest scoring is to play three, six, or nine deals – each player having the same number of turns to deal – then the player with highest cumulative score is declared the winner.

BRIDGE WHIST

This is the same as basic *Whist* in the play, but has a number of complications arising from a different way of deciding trumps.

No trump card is turned. The dealer may name trumps, if he wishes, or he may pass. If he does pass, his partner must name the trump. Any of the four suits may be named trumps, or the player may call 'no trumps', meaning that the hand will be played without a trump suit.

After the trump (or no trump) is named, either opponent may declare 'I double'. After such a double, either member of dealer's side may declare 'I redouble' or 'I double back'. The sides may redouble alternately without limit, until one side quits. Then the cards are played.

After the opening lead, by the player at the left of the dealer, dealer's partner puts his hand face up on the table. The dealer then plays the 'dummy' and his own hand, just as in *Dummy Whist*.

The side winning a majority of the tricks scores each odd trick as follows:

If trumps were	♠	♣	♦	♡	NT
Each odd trick counts	2	4	6	8	10

Each double or redouble that was made multiplies by two the score of the winners.

Points are scored also for honours but are kept separate from points for odd tricks. The side that first reaches 30 in odd tricks wins a game. The side that wins two out of three games wins a *rubber*, and earns a bonus of 100.

The honour count is considerably 'gingered up' over that of *Whist*. At a trump declaration, the honours are the five top trumps. They are scored thus:

Side with three honours or *chicane*,

Multiply odd-trick value by   2

Four honours divided between partners,

Multiply odd-trick value by   4

Four honours in one hand,

Multiply odd-trick value by   8

Four honors in one hand, fifth in partner's,

Multiply odd-trick value by   9

Five honours in one hand,

Multiply odd-trick value by   10

(The direction 'Multiply odd-trick value by ...' gives the amount scored for the honours, which do not affect the scoring of the odd tricks.)

Chicane is a hand without a trump.

At no trump, the honours are four Aces. They are scored:

Side with three Aces	30
Four Aces, divided	40
Four Aces in one hand	100

The Whist Family

If one side wins all thirteen tricks, it scores a bonus of 40 for *grand slam*. For winning twelve tricks, a *little slam*, there is a bonus of 20.

The score is kept on paper. The scoresheet is divided into two halves by a vertical line. All the scores of one side (WE) are entered in the left column, and the scores of the other (THEY) in the right. The sheet is also divided by a horizontal line, somewhat below the middle. Only odd-trick scores are entered 'below the line', and they are accumulated to determine when a game (30) has been won. All other scores go 'above the line'. When the table breaks up, each column is added up to determine the grand total won by each side – for odd tricks, honours, slams, rubbers.

NULLO GAMES

In all nullo games the object of play is to avoid winning tricks, or avoid taking certain cards in tricks. Most of the games are especially easy for children to learn, because they have practically no other rules. Only in *Omnibus Hearts* do we find the added wrinkle that you DO want to win some cards while you DON'T want to win others.

FOUR JACKS (POLIGNAC)

NUMBERS OF PLAYERS: Four, five or six.

CARDS: With four players, thirty-two cards – a full deck with all 2s to 6s discarded. All the cards are dealt; each player thus receives eight.

With five or six players, thirty cards – same as above, but the two black 7s also discarded. Each player receives six or five cards.

THE PLAY: Player at left of the dealer leads first. The hands are played out in tricks. There is no trump suit. Each trick is won by the highest card played of the suit led. The object is generally to avoid winning any Jack. But before the opening lead, any player may announce that he will try to win all the tricks. This is called *capot*.

SCORING: To begin a game, equal numbers of counters are distributed to all players. Payments for Jacks and capot are made into a common pool, which is divided equally among all the players when the game ends. Whenever one player is down to his last counter, all players take equal numbers of counters from the pool.

If capot is announced and made, every other player must

pay 5 counters. But if the capot player fails to win all the tricks, he alone pays 5 counters.

When capot is not announced, the player who takes the Jack of spades (called *polignac*) must pay 2 counters into the pool, and 1 must be paid for each of the other three Jacks.

SLOBBERHANNES

This is much the same as *Four Jacks*, with the difference that what you want to avoid winning are: first trick, last trick, and the Queen of clubs. Each of these costs 1 counter, and if you unluckily take all three you must pay an extra counter, 4 in all.

10. The Hearts Family ...

This is the chief group of nullo games. In all, an object of play is to avoid winning hearts. If you are invited to play 'Hearts' with a group that you have never played with before, you had better ask them to state the rules. Otherwise, you may find yourself playing one game while they play another. The name of the basic game, *Hearts*, is used loosely for all its offspring, but there are many variations of name and in particular *Black Maria* and *Black Lady* often denote games different from either the *Black Lady* or *Hearts* described here.

HEARTS

NUMBER OF PLAYERS: Two to six, but almost always four. Other forms of the game are preferred with more or less than four: *Draw Hearts* for two, *Heartsette* for three, *Domino* and *Cancellation Hearts* for five or six.

CARDS: Each receives thirteen cards. When the cards cannot be divided equally, remove enough deuces from the deck to make the deal come out even. Aces rank highest, above Kings.

THE PLAY: The player at left of the dealer makes an opening lead and the cards are played in tricks. A trick is won by the highest card played of the suit led. There is no trump suit, though hearts are often miscalled 'trumps'. The winner of a trick leads to the next trick.

OBJECT OF PLAY: To avoid winning any heart, or to win all thirteen.

SCORING: To begin a game, equal numbers of counters are distributed to all the players. For each heart he wins, a player must pay 1 counter into a pool. If one player alone took no hearts, he wins the pool. If two or more players took no hearts, they divide the pool. But if all players took hearts nobody wins the pool; it stays on the table as a *jackpot* and becomes part of the pool for the next deal. If one player takes all thirteen hearts, nobody pays. (In this last case, it is customary for all players to *ante* 2 or 3 counters, as agreed, to form a jackpot for the next deal.)

If you do not want to use counters, score with pencil and paper. Each heart taken counts 1 against the player. A game can be ended at any agreed time, and the player with the lowest total score is the winner. The usual method is to charge a player 13 if he wins all the hearts. A good alternative is to deduct 13 (or 26, as agreed) from his score, preserving the principle that a player with a bad hand should have a chance to save himself (or gain) by taking *all* the hearts.

HEARTSETTE

This is an adaptation of *Hearts* to an odd number of players. A widow is dealt face down on the table: four cards with three players; two cards with five players. The rest of the deck is dealt out. The widow is turned face up after the first trick and goes to the winner of that trick. He must of course pay for any hearts it contains.

SPOT HEARTS

This is a variation in cumulative scoring that can be applied to any member of the *Hearts* family. The charges for hearts taken go according to rank: Ace counts 14, King 13, Queen 12, Jack 11, the others, their pip value.

BLACK LADY

This is the best-known game of the *Hearts* family. It is what most people refer to when they speak of 'Hearts'.

NUMBER OF PLAYERS: Three to seven. Best for four, without partnerships.

CARDS: The whole deck is dealt, giving equal hands to all. With more or less than four players, discard an appropriate number of deuces from the deck so the deal will come out even.

THE PASS: After looking at his hand, each player passes any three cards he chooses to the player at his left. He must choose his pass and put it on the table before picking up the three cards passed to him by his right-hand opponent.

THE PLAY: The player at left of the dealer makes the opening lead. The cards are played out in tricks. Aces rank highest. A trick is won by the highest card played of the suit led. The winner of a trick leads to the next trick.

OBJECT OF PLAY: To avoid taking the Queen of spades (called Black Lady, Black Maria, Calamity Jane, etc), to avoid taking hearts, or to take *all* the hearts *and* the Queen of spades.

SCORING: If one player takes all fourteen 'minus' cards, nobody scores. Otherwise, 1 point is charged for each heart won, and 13 points for the Queen of spades. A running total score for each player is kept on paper. The one who first reaches 100 or more loses the game, and the one who has the lowest total at that time wins the game. (To make a shorter game for children, set the limit at 50.)

An alternative method is to score with counters, settling after each hand. Payments are made into a common pool, which is distributed equally to the players from time to time.

CANCELLATION HEARTS

This is a variant for six or more players. Use two decks shuffled together. Deal them out as far as they will go evenly. Put the extra cards face down on the table as a widow. This goes to the winner of the first trick.

The play is as in *Black Lady*. But when two identical cards, such as two Aces of spades, are played on the same trick, they *cancel* each other; they rank as zero and cannot win the trick. Thus, if a deuce is led and all higher cards of the suit played to the trick are paired and so cancelled, the deuce wins.

When ALL cards of the suit led are cancelled, the cards stay on the table and go to the next winner of a trick. The same leader leads again.

The game is scored like *Black Lady*. Counters make for easier scoring than pencil and paper.

DISCARD HEARTS

This is *Black Lady* with the rule that the three cards are passed sometimes to the left and sometimes to the right. (The best plan is to alternate.) The pass often allows you to ruin your neighbour. Alternate passing gives him the chance to get back at you.

OMNIBUS HEARTS

Many regard this as the most interesting game of the *Hearts* family. It is the same as *Black Lady* with one addition – the 10 of diamonds is a 'plus' card, counting 10 *for* you if you win it. Consequently, each suit has its own character – clubs are neutral, diamonds contain the plus card, spades contain the worst minus card, and all the hearts are minus cards. A player who makes a 'take-all' by winning all thirteen hearts, the Queen of spades, and the 10 of diamonds, scores 26 plus.

SKILFUL PLAY: The most dangerous cards to hold are high spades – Ace, King, Queen – without enough lower cards to guard them. Pass such high spades when you are dealt less than three lower spades. Pass high hearts if you can afford to, and if they look dangerous, but two *low* hearts are usually enough to guard them. Any suit outside of spades is dangerous if you have four or more without any card lower than, say, a six. Even a single very low card, two or three-spot, may not be a sufficient guard. Pass one to three cards from the top or middle of such a suit, if you do not have more pressing troubles.

If you do not have any high spades after the pass, lead spades at every opportunity. You can never gather Black Maria by a lower spade lead! You want to try to force her out by spade leads so as to save yourself from winning her by discard. If you have her yourself, usually lead your shortest side suit so as to void your hand of this suit and get a chance to discard Black Maria.

If you are dealt the 10 of diamonds, usually pass it if you can afford to. The 10 is much easier to *catch* than to *save*. It is not often caught by higher diamonds – and even then mostly by accident. It usually falls to the winner of the last trick. The hand with which you may hope to catch it has some Aces and Kings, adequately guarded by lower cards, in two or more suits. Of course, if you hope to catch the 10, don't pass any higher diamonds, and don't ever lead diamonds if you can avoid it. But put a *high* diamond on any diamond lead that might be won by the 10 if you were to play low.

Don't attempt a take-all without a very powerful hand. Certain holdings are fatal no matter how strong you are in other suits – low hearts (not at the end of a long solid suit), the 10 of diamonds (without enough diamond length and strength to save the 10 even if you do not go for take-all). However, such a holding as one or two middling-high hearts is not fatal. You may be able to win the tricks simply by leading these hearts. The players holding higher hearts may shrink from taking the tricks.

When your chief ambition is to avoid taking minus cards, which is most of the time, get rid of your high cards early rather than late. Thus, if you have A, J, 2 in clubs, put the Ace on the *first* club lead and the Jack on the *second*, saving your 2 to escape having to win the more dangerous third lead. The more often a suit is led, the more likely it becomes that Black Maria or hearts will be discarded on it.

BLACK LADY

JOKER HEARTS

The joker is added to the deck. It can be won only by the Ace, King, Queen, or Jack of hearts. Otherwise, it wins any trick to which it is played. If the game is *Heartsette*, an extra card is dealt to the widow. In four-hand basic *Hearts*, the 2 of clubs is discarded so as to keep the deck at fifty-two cards. The joker counts as 1 heart in payment, or, in *Spot Hearts* scoring, 20.

DRAW HEARTS

This is *Hearts* for two players. Each receives thirteen cards. The rest of the deck is placed face down in the centre of the table, forming the stock. The cards are played in tricks. The winner of a trick draws the top card of the stock and his opponent takes the next. After the stock is exhausted, the hands are played out without drawing. The player who takes the fewer hearts wins.

AUCTION HEARTS

The idea of this game is to let the players bid for the privilege of naming the suit to be avoided (that is, the suit that you try *not* to win in the play). *Each* player in turn has one chance to bid, and the highest bidder names the 'minus' suit. A bid is made in terms of the number of counters that the player is willing to pay into the pool. Settlement is made with counters, as in basic *hearts*. If the pool becomes a jackpot, there is no bidding in the next deal. The same player retains the right to name the minus suit, without further payment, until the jackpot is won. This player also makes the opening lead.

DOMINO HEARTS

This is a hilarious game for five or six players. Each receives six cards. The rest of the deck is put face down in the middle of the table, forming the stock. All tricks MUST be composed of cards of the same suit – there is no discarding. When a player is unable to follow suit to the lead, he must draw from the stock until he gets a playable card. After the stock is exhausted, a player unable to follow suit must pass. When a player's hand is exhausted, he drops out of the deal and the others play on. If he should win a trick with his last card, the player at his left leads for the next trick. When all but one have dropped out, the last player must add his remaining cards to his own tricks. Hearts taken are charged at 1 apiece, and the player with the lowest total when another player reaches 31 wins the game.

The End

More fun with Piccolo

Alvin Schwartz
Tomfoolery 30p
Tricks with words to trip you up and muddle your friends.

Witcracks 30p
Jokes of all sorts: riddles, puns, ancient jokes, modern jokes, shaggy dog stories, even 'Confucius say' jokes.

Margaret Gossett
Piccolo Book of Jokes 20p
Q. When is an operation funny?
A. When it leaves the patient in stitches.
There's a groan a minute in this collection of jokes, puns and riddles.

S. B. Cunningham
Piccolo Book of Riddles 20p
A bumper book of riddles from around the world. All the old chestnuts are included as well as a lot of new ones.

Denys Parsons
Fun-tastic! 25p
Even More Fun-tastic! 20p
Two collections of newspaper misprints and howlers, specially selected for children.

Non-fiction

Meredith Hooper
Everyday Inventions   35p

From Coca Cola and the zip to the sewing machine and
television, nearly everything we use has been invented by
someone somewhere . . .

Peter Tunstall
First Feats   25p

Lindberg, Hillary, Magellan, Bell, Leonov – these men all
achieved a 'first' in their chosen field. Fifty exciting stories are
told in this lively anthology.

Jane Sherman **Piccolo Book of
Amazing Scientific Facts** 25p

Do you know . . .
That there is a metal which will melt in your hand?
How a camel stores water inside his body?
What is the fastest-moving creature in the world?
What makes a cobra dance?
Answers to these and many other amazing scientific facts are
given in this fascinating book.

You can buy these and other Piccolo books from booksellers
and newsagents ; or direct from the following address :

Pan Books Cavaye Place London SW10 9PG
Please send purchase price plus 10p postage

While every effort is made to keep prices low, it is sometimes
necessary to increase prices at short notice. Pan Books reserve
the right to show on covers new retail prices which may differ
from those advertised in the text or elsewhere